MW01287317

INSIGHT, INFLUENCE, AND FLOW

INSIGHT, INFLUENCE, AND FLOW

A GUIDE FOR BUSINESS PROFESSIONALS

DAVID WALDAS

Waterside Press

Copyright © 2018 by David Waldas

All rights reserved. Published in the United States of America. No part of this book may be reproduced or transmitted in any form or by any means, graphic, electronic, or mechanical, including photocopying, recording, taping, or by any information storage or retrieval system, without the permission in writing from the publisher.

This edition published by Waterside Press

For information address Waterside Press, Cardiff by the Sea, California.

First Edition
ISBN 978-1-943625-80-2

Library of Congress Cataloging-in-Publication Data (*to come*)

Manufactured in the United States of America

10 9 8 7 6 5 4 3 2 1

*For Tracy, Olivia, and Ava who have
lived in my electromagnetic field as
I fine tuned the Aligned Living process.*

CONTENTS

ACKNOWLEDGMENTS

This book came together through many relationships. While it took a relatively short time to write, the content was created over many years. Every person, whether friend, family member, client, coworker, boss, or teacher that I have interacted with in some way contributed to this knowledge. Every experience we have in some way influences who we are and what we create. I would like to acknowledge several of them here.

First to the concept of being a life long learner. Mastery is a fluid process. It is never about being complete, but rather having the tools to navigate an ever expanding reality as we explore what we are truly capable of.

To my family to which this book is dedicated. They have joined me on this journey of self-development. Sometimes eagerly and other times through a forced expansion that comes from sharing their life (and energetic space) with me. As well as the expansion they have each brought to me. Complacency does not survive long in our household.

To my Aligned Living Clients and Coaches who have provided so many stories and experiences that you will read about in this book. They have been great reflectors as their growth has helped foster my own.

To the pioneers in flow states, in particular Dr. Mihaly Csikszentmihalyi and Dr. Keith Sawyer who have opened these doors to so many of us.

To Bob Petrello a friend and mentor who supported me to believe in myself at whole new levels.

To Phil Kugler my high school photography teacher who showed me what it looks like to be your authentic self in an otherwise conforming environment. He was my first teacher that showed up as his playful self, without a mask, and taught from his heart.

To Cory Cipriani one of my business professors in college who called me on my B.S. My charm was met with accountability. In one three-minute interaction he taught me the value of integrity and hard work over making excuses. While Cory most likely has no memory of that brief interaction or even of me, I have referenced those three minutes repeatedly as a guidepost throughout my life.

To Marisa Moris who followed her intuition to seek me out and introduce me to my publicist Bill Gladstone.

To Bill Gladstone who saw the potential in my work, signed me as a client, and within a couple months presented me with my first book offer.

And finally, to the guidance we are constantly receiving from a higher source.

Thank you.

INTRODUCTION

A s you pick up this book I hope your driving question is, "What can this book do for me?" As a business professional, you have to choose where you put your time and energy. So let me cut right to the chase. We have all experienced how the way we are feeling internally affects our day as well as how people respond to us. Some days we are on fire, everybody is impressed by us, we have the Midas touch. Other days we feel more like lepers infecting whatever comes near us. This is a truth. But if we can identify what is going on with us on our "Midas" days, intentionally recreate it, then learn to sustain it, what then? Then we are in a continuous state of Optimal Flow where we have powerful influence and a shift in perspective that gives us deep insight. We become the leaders that others are jumping at the opportunity to follow.

The information in this book is an access point to that reality. Here is what I can promise you. Within the pages of this book and the free recordings available at insightinfluenceandflow.com is everything you need to make the shift from your current normal day-to-day experience of your life to stepping into an altered state of consciousness known as the Aligned Living Flow State. I have watched hundreds of clients experience this shift. The process is mechanical, repeatable, and sustainable.

About 10 percent of these clients step into their power and never look back. From the moment they make the shift, they let go of their personal fears and utilize their "Midas touch" to thrive in their business and personal lives. There are another 30 percent or so of people that take some time to accept and acclimate to how simple, easy, and effective this work actually is. They may feel the need to relapse into old self-defeating patterns several times, as they learn to trust their ability to sustain the Aligned Living Flow State. About 30 percent of my clients use the AL Flow State more passively—often when the stakes are low and they already feel good. They miss the opportunity to utilize it where it makes the biggest difference. They forget about it in those clutch moments that create the major breakthroughs in our business and personal lives. This keeps them just below their breakthrough points. Honestly, it is difficult to witness the clients that are so close to exercising their greatness but choose to hit the brakes instead of the gas. The final 30 percent are the ones that find their own power and success terrifying and prefer the safety of living a life of anonymity with marginal success and happiness. This group of clients usually finds me through a well-intentioned friend or colleague that wants me to "fix" them. All I can offer these folks is a glimpse into their potential and the planting of a seed that may sprout during a more self-empowered time in their lives.

Which group of clients will you fall into? It may surprise you that past success is not the biggest indicator that this will work for you, but it can definitely help you have the confidence to step into the AL Flow State and sustain it. There are three questions you can ask yourself to see if this will work for you. Are you committed to improving yourself? Are you looking for a path to the next level? Can you put your fears aside in order to grow in ways that will break you through old limitations and patterns? If you truthfully answered yes to these three questions, then things are about to change in your life. Dive in and don't look back!

Note to the Reader:

There is a great deal of information contained in this book, including a variety of exercises to assist you. You will most likely find yourself wanting to revisit these exercises. For this reason, I have also listed them in the appendix in the same order in which they appear in the book for your convenience.

CHAPTER ONE

TRANSFORMATION

Acceptance looks like a passive state, but in reality it brings something entirely new into this world. That peace, a subtle energy vibration, is consciousness.

—Eckhart Tolle
A New Earth: Awakening to Your Life's Purposes

Prior to 2016, if you asked me what my most valuable trait was I would have answered, "Perseverance." The successes in my life were hard ones. I was somebody who constantly pushed forward, believing it was the only way to achieve my goals. While I found satisfaction in this struggle, I could never rest. It was my constant effort that held things together in my life. I had not created a solid foundation or system that could run on its own and support me. Instead, the majority of my energy went into stabilizing and supporting what I was creating.

In the spring of 2016 I had an epiphany. Some would describe it as an intervention from the divine, others would simply say something clicked in me. Regardless, there was a single moment of realization when everything in my life changed. I was on a working vacation with my family driving on I-70 through Vail, Colorado. As we came around the last corner before heading up Vail Pass, I suddenly found myself in the Aligned Living Flow State. In a ten-second period, my whole operating system changed. I instantly knew the steps to recreate this experience and what it would take to maintain it. This epiphany became Aligned Living, a coaching and training business I created to share this technique.

This new technique had nothing to do with perseverance; it had nothing to do with pushing. Those were ways I was trying to change my external world to make my internal world more comfortable. Up to that point, my life had felt like trying to bail the ocean with a five-gallon bucket. It was a never-ending task and the moment I made headway the water would flow back into the ocean. This external push was a fool's errand. There was no way to make the external world a comfortable enough place that my internal world could follow suit.

The truth came in as a simultaneous experience and understanding. The only way to experience the inner comfort and peace I had been seeking was to stop entraining with the chaotic external world and entrain with myself. From this place of internal alignment, it became abundantly clear that anything was possible. When our first priority changes from influencing the external world to aligning our inner world, an instant peace comes in. You may be saying, "I picked up this book to become a more powerful, influential, and successful business person. Why are you talking to me about inner peace?" If it makes you feel more comfortable (or peaceful), you can see the inner peace as a pleasant side effect of this work. I lead with it because it is one of the first things people notice when they start working with the Aligned Living techniques.

Operating from within this balanced internal state is what makes everything else work. As I lost that feeling of discomfort, my drive lost the hint of desperation for change. From this place, my urgency started to disappear. I started to feel more like a veteran that had already achieved his aspirations and did not have anything to prove. I started walking around with the clear understanding that who I am is the proof. I could feel my alignment and authority starting to radiate out from me. It was not something I had to show people, it simply became self-evident as I began being who I truly am. As a pioneer of this technique to access the AL Flow State, it took me close to a year to stabilize in this new operating system. I struggled with how simple the process was. I repeatedly slid back into trying to make it happen and engaging in the external discomfort and struggle. I did not have indisputable proof yet that this actually worked. I was developing the proof by living it and witnessing the experiences of my clients. Throughout that year my trust for the Aligned Living technique grew with each experience.

The more I accepted how powerful and life changing these simple techniques were, the more I allowed them to support me. I moved from pushing my business along, keeping it just viable enough to justify continuing working at it, to thriving in it as opportunity after opportunity started knocking on my door. Prior to this shift, I was the one out continuously knocking on doors (literally, at one point, as a solar energy sales person). As Brendon Burchard says, "When you knock on the door of opportunity, do not be surprised that it is work who answers." I felt like as long as I was out knocking on doors and doing the work that answered, I was making progress. I was so busy doing, that I didn't notice how hard I was working for so little. Once this reversed and opportunities started knocking on my door, I became more selective and started saying "yes" only if it felt in resonance with me.

This reverse in flow, finding myself being sought after, has become the norm now. I realized as I stepped into my alignment, I owned my authority. The moment that happened, people recognized it in me and saw I had something to offer. This is a very different experience than the old push of me trying to sell somebody on myself and what I had to offer. Now my sales pitch is showing up fully aligned and in the AL Flow State.

This book itself is a perfect example of the fruits of Aligned Living. For years I have been "working" at writing a book. I took classes on being a writer and on the publishing process. I went to workshops and entered contests. I pitched my ideas to the connected people I knew. I pushed and got nowhere. People would be interested, but it never came together. Then one day a woman walked into the building where my office was located. We started chatting about what I do, and within minutes she volunteered that she was an author and thought I should be as well. She introduced herself as Marisa Moris, took my card and told me she would tell her publishing agent about me and send an email to connect us. She told me her publishing agent was her good friend Bill. Her "good friend" ended up being Bill Gladstone, one of the more accomplished publishing agents out there. His clients include the likes of *New York Times* best-selling authors Eckhart Tolle, Marie Kondo, Dr. Barbara De Angelis, and Thom Hartmann, to drop a few names. This is the guy that got the first Dummies books published. I wasn't quite ready to accept all this as a truth. Then, twenty minutes later, I received an email connecting us. That weekend I was at Bill and his wife Gayle's house sharing my work with them. We spent about four hours together, and Bill offered to represent me and here we are with my first book published.

I didn't push once to make this happen. In fact, this was only able to happen once I had stopped pushing. Then the opportunity knocked on my door. Of course, work has followed, but it is different. I am not trying to make it happen. I am aligning and allowing it to happen. My story would mean little to you until you know I am not an anomaly. Others have used this same system to create similar shifts in their lives.

Let me introduce you to my client Samantha Skelly. Sam is a successful entrepreneur and the owner and creator of Hungry for Happiness. Her business helps women shift their relationship with food by helping them discover their true passions and what they are really hungry for. Sam, like most of us striving to be successful in the business world, thought the only way to be successful was through force, grit, and hard work. I sat down with Sam and interviewed her shortly after she had completed the Aligned Living six week program for business professionals. She was experiencing amazing shifts in her work and personal life and decided to continue working with me on a weekly basis. What follows is an overview of what Sam shared.

Sam described her biggest challenges coming into this work. She realized so much of her drive to constantly do more through, force, grit, and hard work was driven by fear. She felt like she had to constantly meddle with every aspect of her business and say yes to every opportunity. She was afraid that if she didn't jump on each opportunity, they might stop coming in. She found herself taking on clients and business relationships even if they weren't a right fit.

As Sam started living in the AL Flow State, her perspective and actions quickly changed. "I was afraid my business would fail, so I said yes to everything and always tried to do more. Now that I am in this place of alignment, I have become discerning. Do I feel an energetic expansion when I think about this opportunity? Is it in resonance or is it in dissonance? That is literally how I make decisions now. It feels easy and peaceful. Sometimes this does trigger my ego because the old me thinks it should be harder and more of a struggle."

One of the biggest shifts Sam initially made was letting go of her longtime business manager. Sam really liked her business manager and as a result had been trying to force it to work when it wasn't really a good fit. She shared, "I couldn't see that from my place of fear." Sam was afraid that if she let her business manager go, her whole business would fall apart. From this place of fear Sam was about to offer this business manager profit shares, equity in the company, and a substantial raise, hoping that would motivate her to be a better fit. As Sam spent some time in her A.L. Flow State, she realized she was operating from fear. "I surrendered, let go, and listened to myself." From this place of clarity, the fear fell away. Sam realized how big of a mistake she was about to make and changed direction. She let her business manager and one other employee go and hired two new employees that felt in complete resonance with her and the mission of Hungry for Happiness.

In that first month, Sam worked with her existing and new employees to restructure their sales model. This was something she had wanted to do for a long time but in the past fear had gotten the best of her. She had allowed her old business manager to convince her to stick with their existing systems. The results surpassed any goals they had set. The gross sale for the month moved from $47,000 to $70,000. Sam was amazed, "I used to equate hard work and push and hustle to creating success. Now I am doing this so much less. I understand it is about surrender and right choices and right opportunities. The more I am showing up, aligning, and letting go, the more things truly click. I am in flow. I always had to be in control. It was not about me taking my foot off the break and trusting. It was more like me taking my foot off the clutch and pushing the gas at the same time. It wasn't scary, it was effortless. It went from stalling to fully flowing. I was not focused on how do I not force this. I was only focused on how do I stay present, how do I stay aligned, how do I stay in the AL Flow State. I hone in my energy so I am not distracted and influenced by others, but really listening to myself."

I asked Sam about how this was affecting her relationships. She shared, "Since I started doing this work, my relationship with myself has increased so significantly that it has become blatantly obvious which relationships are a fit in my life and which are not. Then I thought it would be up to me to take action and have the conversations or not about what isn't working. However, I mostly have not needed to. As I disengage from the relationships that I need to, they seem to fade out on their own; it is self-sorting. Or they feel me disengaging and try to get more of my attention and energy. This has shown me so clearly where my energy needs to go and with which people. I can look at a person in my life and no longer make excuses for why the person should be in my world. I used to get caught up in the emotions and let people take me down with them. Now I am so clear about whether I want to engage with them or not."

This is not just about disengaging from relationships; it is primarily about allowing them to shift. Sam had seen powerful results with her existing employees' responses. "As I am getting more clear about what I expect," she related, "my leadership skills have grown so much. I'm clear about what I expect, I communicate it from a place of alignment and power, and my leadership team is either rising up with me or falling off. My business manager had to leave as well as one of our contractors. I have been able to say with great clarity that this is what I expect and this is how we do things around here and I need my team on board with this. My team has a whole new trust and respect for me and this is only two months in. My team members are now way better with communication because I am. They are way better with not needing micromanagement because I am not feeling the need to micromanage them. They are taking higher levels of responsibility and commitment to their work because I expect that from them without micromanaging or meddling. They are more committed to the mission because so am I—and without getting stuck in and messing around with all the irrelevant details."

I asked Sam what the biggest challenges had been in doing this work. She answered, "Letting the people go that are not a fit. It was still hard letting my business manager go even though once we had our conversation, she could see it was not a match too, and it became more of a mutual decision. I used to have a horrible time with boundaries. I wanted everybody to stay and be happy even if they weren't a fit. So, I would adjust to make them comfortable. Now I am better with boundaries in all areas of my life because I am clear about what I want. Interestingly, I don't have to set them very often. The way I am now is teaching other people how to treat me, and they are responding in kind."

I asked Sam if she was experiencing a challenge in reconciling how big the changes are compared to the amount of work she is doing to make them. She responded, "There is a part of me that still struggles with this. I may think, this is too good to be true. Then I see the results and I know it is not. For almost thirty years I have lived in a world of hustle and push to make it happen. Since I have been working with you I have made a substantial behavior shift and my beliefs are slowly catching up. I have made a 100 percent commitment to knowing how important staying aligned is, even when I feel my old beliefs trying to come in and convince me I should be pushing harder. I have had to maintain a self-awareness of what I am doing and connect it to the results I am seeing. I feel like this is a secret weapon for me. I feel like I don't have to question myself in the same ways anymore because when I am in alignment the answers are just there. It has saved me so much time and money, and I am already helping so many more people. I know I don't have to go out searching and meddling for answers. I just go into alignment, and it feels so obvious to me. I was meeting with some business associates the other day who haven't done any of this work yet. As I listened to them, I realized I used to be just like them. They were pushing and pushing, and I could see how exhausted they were. I thought, I have a secret weapon. I am creating so much more without the exhaustion and push and struggle."

It has been a pleasure working with Sam and seeing such spectacular results. She is an extremely self-aware person. This has helped her immensely to stay on track and committed to living in the AL Flow State. This is an area where she really stands out. The baseline information we collected has assisted her with this clarity. I have new clients complete an application to work with me or any of our Aligned Living coaches. This provides a baseline as to where we are operating from and lets us know what they want to change and what they want to create more of. I recommend you take a few minutes to complete this same questionnaire to assist you in monitoring your growth. Once we step into the Aligned Living work, most people's perspectives shift so quickly that they are unable to track it. As a result, they experience a sort of amnesia about how they used to think. Your answers will help you recognize how much you have shifted so you can value the steps you are taking that are creating the new results. When we see the value in something, we are far more likely to stay committed to it. This awareness will also assist you in navigating how differently you present yourself to others. People will respond to your growth. Having an understanding of how much and in what areas you have shifted will be invaluable in understanding others' responses as well as in explaining yourself to them.

Here are the application questions we use at Aligned Living with our six-week programs. It will serve you well to take a few minutes to respond to these questions. This is your only opportunity to record your baseline. Once you begin this work, your perspective will most likely start shifting right away. (You are welcome to complete this application through the Aligned Living web page at www.alignedliving.today/aligned-living-six-week-program-application.) You will automatically be emailed your results.

Aligned Living Six-Week Program Application

Thank you for taking the time to complete this application. Keep in mind there are no wrong answers. This is about getting in touch with where you are operating from right now. Please be open and honest with your answers. They will provide you and your potential coach insight into whether this program is the right fit for you. Any information you share will be treated with the highest level of respect and confidentiality.

Name: _____

What drew you here to work with an Aligned Living coach?

What are your top three challenges in life right now?

What are your top three successes in life right now?

List the three to five most influential relationships in your life right now.

Explain how each relationship feels supporting to you and how it feels challenging to you.

Rate your level of fulfillment on a scale of 1-10 for:

    Home Life:
    Work Life:
    Social Life:

How committed would you describe yourself to your own personal growth?

CHAPTER TWO

NEW BUSINESS PARADIGMS

I came to the conclusion that we should aspire to increase the scope and scale of human consciousness in order to better understand what questions to ask. Really, the only thing that makes sense is to strive for greater collective enlightenment.

—Elon Musk
Quoted on Businessinsider.com, from
Businessweek, September 13, 2012

D ecisive, innovative thinker, highly productive, and powerful influencer—these have become four of the most sought after traits of the new business leader. In this book, I will teach you how to access and use the Aligned Living Flow State to activate your individual genius and become more decisive, innovative, creative, intuitive, and productive. Ultimately, this is a guide to being a powerful influencer, innovator, and next level business leader.

Traditionally, business has always happened in ordinary reality, that rational, logical state of consciousness where good, sound, and responsible decisions are made. This has been the realm of business. There has not been a place here for the dreamy creatives, the people who live in a disconnected world of artistic discovery and expression, floating through life in their non-ordinary reality, never quite able to ground their ideas and create anything meaningful in our ordinary reality. The space cadet zoning out in the back of the classroom was never destined to be the next powerful CEO. Yet recently we are seeing more and more divergent thinkers like Elon Musk, Richard Branson, Google founders Larry Page and Sergey Brin, and founder of Facebook, Mark Zuckerberg, emerging as some of the top business leaders and innovators in the world. They have the reason and logic as well as something else. They have the ability to break existing paradigms, to take dreamy, outlandish ideas and turn them into reality. These new leaders have figured something out. They have found the balancing point between the rational and the dreamy, the practical and the impractical. They have learned how to live and operate from the place where ordinary and non-ordinary reality converge. This book is about how to access that exact place, the state of consciousness known as flow state.

In working with and interviewing business professionals, specific themes have emerged that seem to be of universal concern: a push to be more productive, more motivated, more innovative, and more capable of navigating in a world of constantly changing priorities. As we follow these concerns back to their source, we discover they all originate from a feeling of being squeezed by increasing demands. While this squeeze is not anything new, the speed at which we need to adapt and respond certainly is. Our current technology gives us access to massive amounts of information, and quite often in real time. Not too long ago, we only had a few key variables to adapt to, and we had limited data connected with these variables. As a result of this limitation, we operated in relatively slow-moving business environments. We had time to process, think things through, and adapt to the shifts in our markets.

With the advancements in technology we have constant real-time access to more information and variables than we ever imagined. These variables give us an opportunity to be in a continuous state of monitoring and course correction. There is always more work than can be done, as new data is endlessly pushed at us driving our actions and decisions. Our ordinary, reality-based consciousness can't keep up, and we experience high levels of stress. When people are under stress their thoughts and actions tend to be more reactive and unconscious. Inside this squeeze, their success strategies are not coming from their center.

These challenges have driven an unprecedented interest in accessing non-ordinary reality and more importantly operating in an ultimate flow state, on that razor's edge between ordinary and non-ordinary realities. While non-ordinary reality is not a difficult place to access, balancing on the edge between realities has been an elusive endeavor—until now.

The flow state access points that have been available have taken a great deal of commitment, training, and/or risk. This has left many of us itching for a practical access point into flow, as well as a way to sustain it. *Insight, Influence, and Flow* will give you that access and teach you the skills you can implement to sustain it. I use the term Aligned Living Flow State (AL Flow State) in my system to differentiate this work, particularly in reference to the simple, repeatable steps we take to access AL Flow State. In the business world, it is surprisingly common for people to reach non-ordinary states through the use of pharmacology, starting the day with drugs and re-dosing throughout the day. The commonly accepted use of caffeine and nicotine is being supplemented at alarming levels with amphetamine-based "smart drugs" like Adderall. For many business professionals, at the end of the day when it is time to unhook and go to sleep, powerful sleeping pills have become part of their bedtime routine.

We are pushing our bodies in unhealthy and unsustainable ways in attempts to keep up.

Many people are seeking these heightened states and clarity through exercise and/or traditional meditation. These approaches, while far healthier, can be time-consuming, and the results take a much bigger commitment to achieve. While the techniques taught in this book may fall within the description of meditation, the process and outcome are in a category of their own.

We need a healthy and sustainable way to keep up with the pace of business today. Squeezing others and pushing ourselves harder is a natural reaction to the shifting demands of the current business environment, but obviously it's not the long-term answer. We have an unprecedented demand, calling us to adapt our normal state of consciousness. The only way to thrive in this "squeeze" is by living in the AL Flow State. This book is the roadmap; it makes this next-level human state available to anybody who is committed to achieving it.

Before we get into the process this book lays out, I want to share a little bit about who I am and where my perspective comes from. I am an executive coach and have assisted hundreds of clients to discover their greatness and thrive in their lives. I created Aligned Living, which is a system that teaches clients how to access the AL Flow State and learn to utilize this state of consciousness to excel in their pursuits.

My career path has unfolded in a unique way, setting me up to become an expert in accessing flow state and in teaching this access to my clients. I have pursued a variety of careers leading me up to this point. I spent a combined ten years in the business field in management, sales, and entrepreneurship, as a small business owner and manager. Additionally, I spent twelve years as a middle and high school teacher, and three years as a varsity boys' soccer coach. My passion for combining my business and educational experience with my deeply intuitive nature launched me into a successful career as an executive coach and workshop leader, which I have been pursuing for the past seven years.

While my work experience plays an undeniable role in what I bring to my clients, there is something else that really prepared me for this career. I was born with the ability to think outside of the box naturally—but had to face the challenges that accompanied that. I spent many years training myself to understand and integrate into the main stream. Through a long series of trials, navigating through many successes and a healthy dose of wisdom-building failures, I found the access point to the AL Flow State. It has become my passion to teach others how to live and operate in this space.

I came into this world as a dreamy kid, the highly intelligent creative that just didn't fit into the existing structures. I seemed to live in a different place, not the ordinary reality the world generally operated in, but rather a non-ordinary reality. I was stuck in the big picture and the finite details for many years, challenged in navigating the middle ground that would eventually connect me to the rest of the world. My early learning demonstrated this. I was able to read, but couldn't tell my teachers the letters in the words or the sounds they made. I struggled with counting, but could do simple addition and subtraction. This became a theme in my life. It was as if I had the answers but couldn't figure out the questions. In a world full of questions, this ability had great potential, but was of little use until I learned how to integrate it into ordinary reality.

Through the conditioning of society and schooling, I slowly figured out how to navigate in ordinary reality. I was able to achieve in this realm in a rather average way. There was always the idea that something was wrong, I definitely was not living up to my potential. Once I learned to live in the ordinary reality the majority of the world shared, I would often let go of the dreamy state of consciousness I was born into. Why would I hang onto something that had made my life so difficult to navigate? It felt like a liability. It never occurred to me that I could have access to both states of consciousness simultaneously. They felt like they had to be mutually exclusive.

As I developed my abilities in both the ordinary and non-ordinary states of consciousness, my two worlds began showing signs of integration. The gap between the world of questions and the world of answers didn't seem so big. This is how I found access to the AL Flow State. I jumped back and forth between the two states of consciousness until I was eventually able to live on the cusp between them—the Holy Grail of consciousness, the Aligned Living Flow State.

Through my life experience of learning to navigate these unique experiences of reality, I developed the skill set to help others who were stuck in the mainstream to access the world I was born into. Through meditation and visualizations, I found I could show others this pathway. It became very clear that while the two states of consciousness each had something to offer, the goal was really to achieve the balanced state on the cusp of these two realities, the AL Flow State.

I have now dedicated my career to teaching this access point. I have a vision of how the world can evolve, as more and more of us live in the AL Flow State and the natural shift in perspective that comes with it.

The first part of this book focuses on the background information and framework to support you in understanding what we are seeking in the AL Flow State, why we want to achieve it, and the steps to getting there. The second part of this book offers applications of the AL Flow States in different areas of your professional and personal lives as well as guidance in how to navigate in this new way of being.

CHAPTER THREE

FLOW STATES

Meditation is the dissolution of thoughts in Eternal awareness or Pure consciousness without objectification, knowing without thinking, merging finitude in infinity.
—Sivananda Saraswati
Hindu spiritual teacher

stuaries, like the Mississippi Delta, provide some of the most fertile and ecologically diverse locations on Earth. They are created where fresh water rivers flow into the sea. This provides a natural habitat for freshwater, brackish, and saltwater species to all live and thrive side by side. Estuaries have long been the most sought after places to create settlements and thriving communities. New Orleans sits on the Mississippi Delta giving it access to shipping lanes, fresh water for drinking, and a concentration of food sources that can only be found in estuaries. The Hudson River estuary was the settlement place for many Native Americans for the same reasons. This place they called "the River that flows two ways" provided an abundance of natural resources. Estuaries are the one place on Earth where we can access both freshwater and saltwater at the same time, thereby creating unique opportunities.

Estuaries make the perfect metaphor for flow states. They are a balancing point between the world of the freshwater and saltwater ecosystems. They are the brackish water that can only be accessed where these two worlds converge. The AL Flow State is the estuary of consciousnesses. It is the place we can only access when we allow ourselves to loosen our grip on ordinary reality just enough that we can access non-ordinary reality without slipping into it.

The concept of flow states is by no means a new one. People have always accessed these states of consciousness. Humankind's fight-or-flight survival instinct may have been our first access to flow states. The world of flow states is most often tied into sports, particularly extreme sports. These super athletes use the rush and physical danger of the activity to throw them into flow. This book takes a different approach. There is another access point besides jumping off a thousand-foot cliff in a wingsuit. While these activities obviously do the trick, they come at quite a potential cost and require skill sets that the majority of us do not possess. These athletes access a flow state that opens in a small window of time and provides an afterglow of euphoria that carries them through for a day or two. In order to keep achieving this state the athletes need to keep pushing themselves to the next level. Unfortunately, for many of our extreme athlete heroes this has been a fatal chase. When your access point to flow requires you to push your limits, the better you get the further out your limits go. Eventually you are going to find the place you max out. For these super athletes, this often occurs with horrific results.

The reason most of these athletes continue with this cycle has a lot to do with their hardwiring. There is something in them that seeks out continuous stimulus. Once they experience the high of being in flow and the afterglow that follows, everyday life tends to become unbearable. When they have tasted that euphoria, the natural response is to want more. So many of these adventure athletes find their day-to-day life a struggle and live for their next opportunity to reaccess the high of flow. As they push their limits, even the thought of death feels less horrible in comparison to suffering in the consciousness everyday life provides.

While there is no doubt that if you and your coworkers skip the next business meeting and go skydiving together instead you will see some powerful changes, including new levels of creativity and bonding, these extreme examples have little to do with the process we utilize to access flow. I assure you that this book will not put your life in danger. It will, however, threaten old paradigms in the areas of your life where your thinking is blocking you from your greatness. The flow state we will be working with is sustainable. It is not a peak and valley kind of experience. You will learn to bring yourself to the top of your game and maintain this level of consciousness. It is not something you rise to, but rather a place you live in.

Essentially flow states are an experience of consciousness where we feel ourselves letting go of "control" and moving into seemingly effortless action. We instinctively know what to do and do it without thought or processing. For even a reasonable person who is not overly cautious this may sounds a bit irresponsible or even dangerous to practice in your everyday life. The manner in which many people outside of the world of sports are working with the concept of intentionally being in flow only supports that assertion. There is a big difference between flowing in life and accessing or living in an ultimate flow state. Flow states have become of great interest and intrigue to many on a path of personal development. There are countless videos out there of people demonstrating their flow states and giving advice on how to step into yours. They talk about letting go and trusting yourself. There is a push to move away from analysis and resistance and to let your intuition take you down your path.

This thinking begs us to ask: then what is the difference between unconscious behavior and being in flow? Well, unfortunately, there is often little difference in the way it is commonly utilized and taught. Why don't we trust ourselves in the first place? Why do we feel the need to monitor ourselves so closely? For most of us, the answer has had to do with the feedback we have gotten from the world. We may have created things we didn't mean to create, upset people, been misunderstood, or misrepresented ourselves. We decided we couldn't trust ourselves to just let it fly. We decided we needed oversight, and we started scrutinizing, planning, and monitoring ourselves. Most of us have taken this self-oversight way too far. We could probably function far more effectively with a fraction of this restraint. At the same time, we can't ignore that there is a reason we didn't fully trust ourselves in the first place. Most of us operate in a day-to-day level of consciousness that is not exactly stable or of our highest state. We have all had times when we know we shouldn't trust ourselves to operate without self-monitoring, but what level of alignment with self do we need to reach before fully trusting ourselves is a good idea?

When we take our normal state of consciousness and simply take the brakes off, we do end up in a flow state of sorts but definitely not an ultimate flow state. If this is how you have been accessing a flow state, take a minute to be honest with yourself. How has this been working for you? What have you been creating? What have you been breaking apart? My guess is that your answer is a mixed bag—some good, and some not so good.

Here is what sets the AL Flow State apart. The first step in accessing the AL Flow State is to bring ourselves into an aligned state of consciousness. We enter a place where our perspectives shift quite dramatically. We see ourselves and everything in our lives differently. We see the connections, the perfection, and we know we can trust ourselves. From this state of consciousness it feels natural to take your foot off the brake and move into a flow state. We move out of the unconscious behavior that often occurs in pseudo flow states and into the AL Flow State.

There are clear reasons why accessing the AL Flow State is so alluring. We become decisive in a way we have never known before. We are able to make clear decisions without hesitation, and we move outside of emotional responses that would push us to put the desires of others over what is in alignment for ourselves. I continually observe clients in total amazement that they know with crystal clarity which direction to take and just as importantly which directions not to take. They have experiences again and again where they can step forward with a knowing and confidence they couldn't access before. I have heard from many of them some variation of, "I never thought I would choose that, and I am so glad I did. That choice set me up for successes I never imagined accomplishing." From this state of consciousness we think bigger and in more alignment with ourselves and therefore create bigger, more aligned, and more sustainable outcomes.

The intuitive knowing that we access when we are fully in the AL Flow can best be described as a "black box." There is often an instant answer that our brain simply knows. It is as if a supercomputer is receiving input and spitting out answers to questions our conscious minds may not have even fully formed yet. We don't have much awareness of what is happening inside that "black box" or what is even being fed into it. But we do have access to the guidance and answers that are coming out. At first, this feels surreal and you would expect most people to be hesitant trusting this sense of knowing. Quite the contrary happens however. The clarity overrides the self-doubt. Then as we follow our new intuitive and instinctual guidance, the evidence of success quickly builds and another new level of confidence and self-trust manifests. We start to let go of the "why" and "how" questions. These questions have prevented us from keeping up with the speed of life and business, especially the sheer volume of information and variables that are constantly coming at us today. We find ourselves operating in synchronicity with the information, flowing in it rather than being overwhelmed and drowning in stimulus.

I know this sounds a bit outrageous, yet this is the experience our clients are repeatedly having. There is a reason so many people are working with these techniques. If the successes and breakthroughs weren't happening and continuing to happen, people would lose interest and move on to the next distraction. Our clients are sticking with this because it is changing their lives. They are learning to live in the estuary of consciousnesses known as the Aligned Living Flow State.

CHAPTER FOUR
ENTRAINMENT

The human being is a self-propelled automaton entirely under the control of external influences. Willful and pre-determined though they appear, his actions are governed not from within, but from without. He is like a float tossed about by the waves of a turbulent sea.

—Nikola Tesla
"How Cosmic Forces Shape Our Destinies,"
New York American, Feb. 7, 1915

Entrainment is an often unconscious function of our bodies aligning or synching up with external stimulus. This happens at all levels, including neurophysiologically (our nervous system functions by aligning with others' systems or external stimulus) and emotionally (our emotions aligning with others' emotions). We see examples of this everywhere. It plays a role in every human interaction we have, every group or team we are a part of, and every stimulus we come in contact with. We see the deliberate use of entrainment in advertising and social media. While this paints a bleak picture of a loss of sovereignty and indi-viduality, rest assured, it is not so black and white. Throughout this book, we will examine ways to operate outside of the local influence of constantly fluctuating invitations to entrain with other people and situations. We will also examine how entrainment works in the positive, allowing teams to work together in synchronicity at incredible levels. We will learn to live outside of the influence Nikola Tesla described in the quote above.

Electromagnetic Fields (EMF)

In May of 2014, a study was published in the scientific journal *Nature* focusing on the migration of the European robin. Scientists were studying abnormalities in their migration through metropolitan areas. They discovered that very low AM frequencies were disrupting the birds' abilities to navigate as they normally do, using the earth's electromagnetic field (EMF). In essence, the robins were unknowingly entraining with the local AM signals instead of the earth's EMF. These tiny birds are hardwired to pick up the strongest EMF signal. They don't seem to possess the ability to differentiate one EMF from another. In an attempt to solve this problem, scientists constructed small metal windowless houses for the birds. These houses worked as Faraday cages, blocking the local EMFs. This allowed the birds to regain their "compass" and return to a normal migration route.[1]

Animals behaving in unnatural ways have been used to predict potential problems for humans throughout our history. The term "canary in the coal mine" has become a term we use to describe the first subtle indicators that a bigger problem is coming. This expression originated in a very literal way. As coal miners worked deep in the earth, suffocation from oxygen deficiencies was a real problem. Long before electronic sensors to monitor oxygen levels were available, miners brought canaries in

---

1   Morrison, Jessica. 2014. "Electronics' noise disorients migratory birds: Man-made electromagnetic radiation disrupts robins' internal magnetic compasses." *Nature*.

cages down into the mines with them. These birds are far more sensitive to oxygen levels than humans. By simply keeping an eye on the birds, miners could tell if there were any fluctuations in oxygen levels that the far less sensitive humans wouldn't feel until it was too late.

The abnormalities in migratory animals have been showing us that their ability to connect with the EMF of the earth is being disrupted by our urban growth and advances in technology. We are seeing greater numbers of animals' migratory paths and behaviors being altered. While this can be credited to both global climate changes as well as the EMFs of our electronic technologies, it is the latter that we are interested in here.

While the earth has its own electromagnetic field, so do the electronics we use every day, as well as every living thing on this planet. As humans, we are obviously not as sensitive as the European robin or affected in the same way, but to pretend that it has no effect on us is rather naive, even arrogant. This will make greater sense as we examine the study below.

We are each experiencing an enormous number of factors that influence our behavior. Our lives are not lived in a vacuum (or a Faraday cage). Every situation and person pushes and pulls us to think and behave in different ways. Much of this is happening outside of our conscious awareness. One of the most telling examples of this is an experiment conducted by Chris Berka at the renowned ESADE business school in Barcelona, Spain. The goal was to create reliable and repeatable techniques for identifying "emergent leaders." For their study, they attached EEG and HRV monitors to a group of thirty-five MBA students and gave them a case study to solve. They found that they could reliably predict who would become the biggest influencers and leaders in the group within the first thirty minutes. This conclusion was not derived by the participants' outward behavior, but rather by their internal neurophysiological responses. The future leaders had a greater ability to regulate their own nervous systems than other participants. This resulted in an entraining process, where the other students' neurophysiology ended up aligning with the emerging leaders.[2]

If your vital signs involuntarily adjust to align with those of who you consciously or unconsciously decide is the leader in the room, it is not a big jump to accept that this also affects your decision-making. In essence, we defer our own sense of authority to others. While it is a valuable skill to be a team player, letting go of your own sense of autonomy and authority and deferring to others can be disempowering and diminish what you bring to the team and your work.

We have the ability to sense at some level what is happening around us and, as a result, we unconsciously either align or separate from what we are experiencing. We react to the push and pull we feel in our proximity, and we present ourselves differently depending on the situation and who is nearby. Of course, there are the obvious causes that drive this, including emotions, personalities, risks, anxiety, and potential payoffs, but it doesn't stop there. Those factors can't be fully responsible for our neurophysiological shifts of entraining with the "leader" of the group." There must be something more going on. Additionally, if members of the group were entraining with the "emerging leader," what was the leader entraining with? Where was this greater sense of self coming from? How were they able to align with themselves and their own authority? How were they able to be the influencer rather than the one being influenced? There are multitudes of possible answers to these questions. It could have been driven by their ego, experience, faith, training, or any number and

---

2 Wheal, Steven Kotler and Jamie. 2017. *Stealing Fire: How Silicone Valley, The Navy Seals, and Maverick Scientists are Revolutionizing the Way We Live and Work.* New York: HarperCollins Publishers Inc.

combination of these and other variables. While these factors all play contributing roles in the process, throughout this book you will be guided through a step-by-step approach to developing your own awareness system that works for you. You will be given the tools to become the influencer and gain the ability to emerge as the leader.

While science does not fully understand what is happening in the entraining process, it does seem to be tied to our electromagnetic fields. The shifts you will be creating within yourself will give you a great deal of awareness and control over this process. Low AM frequencies may have little effect on us as humans compared to the European robin, but something else is having a huge effect on us. We are entraining with the EMFs of the situations we are embedded in, or what we are focusing on (local or nonlocal), as well as the EMFs of those we perceive as the most powerful around us. These situations and leaders are setting our trajectories forward in life, "like a float tossed about by the waves of a turbulent sea."

What Are You Entraining with?

It is easy in the world to live after the world's opinion; it is easy in solitude to live after our own; but the great man is he who in the midst of the crowd keeps with perfect sweetness the independence of solitude.

—Ralph Waldo Emerson
Self-Reliance and Other Essays

Our electromagnetic field (EMF) is constantly picking up data and then entraining with it at many different levels. We are usually most aware of what is in our immediate physical surroundings and therefore give it the highest priority and most influence. At the same time, we have all had experiences where we were much more focused on something separate from our physical location. Maybe we had an argument with a family member and we were still focusing on unresolved feelings connected to it and continued entraining with that interaction. As humans, we tend to have our emotions driving our experiences. We are usually aware of this at some level, but these emotions also drive and embed in our EMF. We live in a constantly shifting soup of EMFs. It is challenging enough to navigate the influence of other people's EMFs, now technology has only added to this challenge by polluting our EMF with electronics like cell phones, Wi-Fi, and smart meters. I suppose we could all create Faraday cages to operate in much like scientists did for the European robin. But unless you are ready to wear a tinfoil hat to work, we need to look for better options.

The weaker an EMF is, the more influence other EMFs have on it. This leads us to the obvious value of strengthening our own EMF. This alone will do little more than make us better warriors. There will always be a bigger, badder warrior showing up at some point. There is another factor that gives us even more control, while at the same time assisting us in strengthening our own EMF.

The size of our awareness is constantly fluctuating. This usually happens through unregulated emotional reactions to external stimuli. You may be going through your day just fine, feeling good. Then, ding, a text message comes in. Somebody wants something from you that you don't want to give. Instantly you are triggered, emotions of resentment, frustration, judgment, and anger come in. Your awareness shifts from the bigger picture of aligning with enjoyable aspects of your day. You entrain with these new emotions brought on by a simple text message from a person who may normally play a small role in your life. You shift your awareness and zoom in, you let go of the greater picture, and within seconds your whole experience changes. You become angry and feel the need to defend yourself.

The truth is, it is already too late. The threat has already played out. The damage has already occurred. You mistakenly thought the threat was the person asking something of you. In truth, that probably could have been dealt with in ten seconds with a simple reply. The real threat was to your inner balance, your emotional stability, your enjoyment of the moments in your day. When we become aware of what we are entraining with, we take back this power.

We can choose to stay entrained with something far bigger than ourselves. Through our awareness, almost everything can become small stuff. We won't get fooled into shrinking our awareness and creating the temporary illusion that a simple text message is our whole reality. When we maintain the bigger picture, ironically, we are able to be much more present with the moment and our current surroundings. It's easier to connect with the present when there is no longer an emotional threat or something we need to guard against. These negative occurrences lose their ability to upset us in the same way.

Our intelligence and ability to self-regulate give us an option the European robin didn't have. We can be conscious in choosing what we entrain with. Our natural response has been to entrain with the most internally stable person in the room. This only makes sense on a micro level. If you have the freedom to choose what you entrain with, why not entrain with the biggest, most aligned, stable, and powerful EMF? That of the earth. I want to acknowledge that for those of you living a religious or spiritual life, this thinking may feel limited. If this is the case for you, I invite you to expand this model to include the influence of the divine aligning the earth's EMF. As we align with the earth's EMF, we are simultaneously aligning ourselves with the flow of a greater power. Whatever your belief system is, the goal is to align with your highest aspect of self by entraining with something that is stable, nonlocal, and in alignment with the greater picture.

The earth's EMF is not without fluctuations driven by events like solar flares, but it does do pretty well in comparison to the EMFs of your office mates. There are extensive studies about the human connection with the earth's EMF. We will examine these ideas in the next chapter as we explore Schumann resonance and coherence theories.

CHAPTER FIVE

SCHUMANN RESONANCE AND COHERENCE THEORIES

To modern science, because we are conditioned to believe that we are separate from our world, there is nothing that allows for that connection and that influence. So to us, we call it a miracle, but it is only a miracle until we understand the connection and then it becomes a technology.

—Gregg Braden
Author of New Age literature

Schumann resonance is the natural frequency of the earth's electromagnetic field. While science is not clear on the degree of the relationship between humans and Schumann resonance, it is now being accepted that there is one. This relationship is often explained through the concept of coherence theories, the idea that all things are connected and move in concert with each other. In this chapter we will examine the effects this has on us. We will also look at how we can either continue to entrain with our local surroundings or intentionally open our awareness to entrain with ourselves and the far more stable, nonlocal resonance of the earth's EMF.

We have had some incredible pioneers compiling new information in the field of coherence theory and sharing it with the world, including the HeartMath Institute, Gregg Braden, and Dr. Joe Dispenza. The HeartMath institute is a nonprofit that has been around for over twenty-five years. Their scientific research has demonstrated that the heart does far more than pump blood through the body. They have "explored the physiological mechanisms by which the heart and brain communicate and how the activity of the heart influences our perceptions, emotions, intuition and health.[3]" From their inception, they have had a fascination with understanding why emotions are felt in the physical body around the area of the heart. They conducted some of the first research studying how both stressful emotions and positive emotions affect the autonomic nervous system as well as the hormonal and immune systems.

Braden, a former aerospace engineer who has done a great deal of work with the HeartMath Institute, believes that science has discovered what ancient cultures have been practicing for many years—that there is a connection between our hearts and our brains. When these two organs come into synchronicity with each other, we call it heart-brain coherence. In a talk he gave on YouTube, Braden describes how science's new discoveries have changed what we know about the relationship between the heart, the brain, and the body. It has always been thought that the brain was the master control of our body. Science believed that the brain gave all the orders, that it was the "master organ." Recently we have discovered that the heart and brain are in constant communication with each other through very low frequency signals, and it is the heart that is actually sending the majority of the signals

---

3   Rollin McCraty, Ph.D. 2015. *Science of the Heart: Exploring the Role of the Heart in Human Performance Volume 2.* Boulder Creek, CA: HeartMath Institute.

to the brain, triggering the brain to release whatever chemicals are called for into the body. It is, in fact, the intelligence of the heart that is driving the neurochemical releases in our body of neurotransmitters like dopamine, serotonin, and endorphin.

If you are not familiar with these neurotransmitters, here is a quick overview. Dopamine is the body's reward system and gives pleasurable sensations. Serotonin is a natural mood stabilizer. It reduces depression and regulates anxiety, libido, and appetite. It is also related to how we operate when taking power over others and in being submissive. Endorphins allow us to block pain and in intense situations access incredible strength and stamina. They are a natural opiate and can create feelings of euphoria and an overall better mood. Looking at these few examples of our neurotransmitters, you can imagine how important this communication is between the heart and the brain.

In the studies conducted by the HeartMath Institute they found that heart rate variability was "the most dynamic and reflective indicator of one's emotional states and, therefore, current stress and cognitive processes.[4]" This was a clear indicator that taxing emotions such as frustration caused the higher level brain centers and autonomic nervous system to function less smoothly. They moved into disorder, negatively affecting heart rhythms and nearly the entire bodily system. This discovery led scientists into a breakthrough understanding of the bidirectional communication pathways between the heart and brain. They realized that the heart had its own neural network (essentially its own brain) and significantly influences how we perceive and interact with everything we encounter. "Numerous studies have since shown that heart coherence is an optimal physiological state

---

4   Rollin McCraty, Ph.D. 2015. *Science of the Heart: Exploring the Role of the Heart in Human Performance Volume 2.* Boulder Creek, CA: HeartMath Institute.

associated with increased cognitive function, self-regulatory capacity, emotional stability and resilience.[5]" Study in the field of neurocardiology has proven that the heart does indeed have its own complex neural network. In other words, the heart has its own brain. In 1991 Dr. J. Andrew Armour introduced the term "heart-brain" for the intrinsic cardiac nervous system of the heart. This heart-brain is made up of the same intricate neural circuitry (complex ganglia, neurotransmitters, proteins, and support cells) as the cranial brain. It also has the ability to operate separately from the cranial brain with its own memory (both short and long term), learning capacity, and the ability to feel, sense, and make decisions. The cranial brain and heart-brain are in communication with each other. Shockingly, the heart-brain actually sends more information to the cranial brain than it receives. Our heart has its own separate intelligence.

These two functioning brains in our body have the ability to work together in "coherence," or to work against each other. Coherence is a psychophysiological state where we experience smooth and stable heart rhythms and an improvement in our mental perception, intuitive awareness, and overall performance. This heart-brain and cranial brain coherence is the science behind the AL Flow State, and the key to achieving it.

The HeartMath Institute has conducted numerous studies about coherence. Many of these studies are based on the role emotions play. One study involving hundreds of subjects had each participant connect with and intentionally feel positive emotions. What they found is that as each person moved into a positive emotional state their hearts responded with a smoother and more stable rhythm, creating a greater degree of coherence.

---

5 Rollin McCraty, Ph.D. 2015. *Science of the Heart: Exploring the Role of the Heart in Human Performance Volume 2.* Boulder Creek, CA: HeartMath Institute.

The study found the results to be even more significant if the subject had just been experiencing negative emotions.

From the HeartMath Institute's work, we can take away several understandings. First, the psychophysical state of coherence where our heart and brain are working together opens us up to a flow state. Second, positive emotions bring us into coherence and negative emotions bring us out of coherence. The next logical deduction is that the more control we have over the emotions we are internally experiencing, the more we can choose to be in coherence, thus making it easier to access the AL Flow State. We will come back to this deduction later in the book as we access the AL Flow.

What we have been talking about is our internal state of being. For most people, this information naturally makes sense and logically expands on what they already know about their internal emotional state and how it affects their ability to function. These next findings tend to blow people's minds. Unfortunately, science is reluctant to change and expand on old established theories. New data is often ignored if it does not support or corroborate what science has already established as "truth." What follows is an expansion beyond the science that shows up in textbooks. Keep in mind, these findings have been proven repeatedly in multiple scientific experiments.

Coherence theory goes on to examine the effect our EMFs have on our surroundings. This is the science that explains entrainment. Our EMFs, as the name suggests, are made up of both our electric field as well as our magnetic field. Both our brains and our hearts put out EMFs. The electric fields produced by our hearts are about sixty times greater than those produced by our brains, and the magnetic field of our hearts are more than one hundred times stronger than that of our brains. Our hearts have by far the biggest impact on our EMF.

Electrical and magnetic influences are constantly affecting every cell in our bodies and therefore every biological system in our bodies. Our bodies operate internally through signals in the form of electrical and hormonal impulses mainly generated by the heart and brain. The type of impulse and the patterns of spacing between those impulses carry information. This is how our body internally regulates and communicates with itself. The HeartMath institute takes this theory to the next level. They believe that our external EMFs affect our surroundings and the people in it.

> The low-frequency oscillations generated by the heart and body in the form of afferent neural, hormonal and electrical patterns are the carriers of emotional information and the higher frequency oscillations found in the EEG reflect the conscious perception and labeling of feelings and emotions. We have proposed that these same rhythmic patterns also can transmit emotional information via the electromagnetic field into the environment, which can be detected by others and processed in the same manner as internally generated signals.[6]

This would explain how the participants in Chris Berka's emerging leader study conducted at the ESADE School of Business in Barcelona, Spain, entrained with the emerging leaders. Whether this theory is 100 percent accurate is less relevant than the understanding that our internal nervous system is the wiring that carries this electrical and hormonal information throughout our bodies. Our ability to influence and be

---

6 Rollin McCraty, Ph.D. 2015. *Science of the Heart: Exploring the Role of the Heart in Human Performance Volume 2.* Boulder Creek, CA: HeartMath Institute.

influenced, however, doesn't stop there. We also transmit and receive "wirelessly" through our EMFs. Just as our heart and brain are in constant communication with each other in our internal systems, our EMF is constantly in communication with the EMFs of whatever and whoever are externally around us.

The HeartMath Institute has developed equipment to help us study coherence at a global level. They are creating twelve ultra-sensitive magnetic field detectors and installing them around the globe. This project, known as the Global Coherence Initiative or GCI, is partially completed and continuously monitors the earth's magnetic resonance. They are operating with four primary hypotheses that they share on their webpage: "1. Human and animal health, cognitive functions, emotions and behavior are affected by planetary magnetic and energetic fields. 2. The earth's magnetic fields are carriers of biologically relevant information that connects all living systems. 3. Each individual affects the global information field. 4. Large numbers of people creating heart-centered states of care, love and compassion will generate a more coherent field environment that can benefit others and help offset the current planetarywide discord and incoherence.[7]"

What they are finding is that there is a feedback loop between the EMFs of living beings on the planet and the EMF or Schumann resonance of the earth. The most fascinating part of this idea is that this feedback loop works in both directions. Not only does the Schumann resonance of the earth affect its inhabitants, but our internal coherence also affects the resonance of the earth. The more people that regulate their internal states and maintain a high level of heart-brain coherence, the greater the coherence of the earth. The earth then feeds this coherence back onto the planet and assists in moving each of us, particularly those who are not self-regulating, into a more coherent state. In

---

7   2018. *HeartMath Institute*. Accessed October 12, 2017. www.heartmath.org.

theory, as we are living in the AL Flow State we are not just assisting those whose EMFs directly overlap our own, we are feeding our coherence into the global EMF and assisting all of humanity. This is a powerful concept to digest. As more and more data is being generated each day that supports this as truth, it is closer to being widely accepted as reality.

CHAPTER SIX

SOVEREIGNTY

The distinguishing characteristics of mind are of a subjective sort; we know them only from the contents of our own consciousness.

—Wilhelm Wundt
Principles of Physiological Psychology (1902)

Sovereignty is often an illusion. Most people have no idea how much they are influenced by others. In chapters four and five, we explored how science supports this idea through the concepts of entrainment and coherence theories. In this chapter, we will move from theory into examining the role sovereignty is currently playing in our lives. We will also be doing some exercises to experience a greater degree of sovereignty. Sovereignty is about operating outside of the influence of others. While 100 percent sovereignty may not be a possibility or even desirable, it is clear that most people operate with very little sovereignty at all.

Let's take a minute to look at the levels of sovereignty of the people you work with. Think of five people that you work with. They could be a part of a team, clients, customers, or management. How they are connected to you is not relevant. Pick people that you interact with regularly. I would bet that with a fairly high degree of accuracy you could estimate the level of influence the people around them have on each of these individuals, and would be able to put them in order from the highest level of sovereignty to the least.

Give it a shot, go ahead and order these five people now. Which of these individuals' traits did you use to order them? Here are some of the common indicators people use: confidence/arrogance, pleaser/brownnoser, leader, follower, easily influenced, influencer, their job title, level of success, and personal power. Now insert yourself into the list. Where do you classify yourself? As you examine your list, who do you see as a role model and admire the most? Who do you find the most challenging to work with? Many people find there is a sweet spot in their list of people where a high level of sovereignty exists that ties into confidence. However that admiration can be derailed by arrogance. Do you see the connection between how influential people are and their ability to operate in a more sovereign way? Do you see the lack of interest most people have in following the less sovereign as well as how perceived arrogance can be a detractor from their influence?

So much of people's behavior is guided by insecurity and emotion. Moving into a more sovereign state of consciousness has a very interesting effect on our emotions. Have you noticed how the people that you placed on the less sovereign end of your list seem to be more affected by the emotions of others? They are more likely to entrain with the emotions of people they are connected to, whether through relationships or proximity. As we work with the following visualization, the more this describes you, the more profound this initial shift will most likely be for you. If you see yourself as somebody who does not pick up on others' emotions it will still be beneficial to participate in the visualization exercises in the recording for this chapter. You may be surprised by how much of a shift you feel. We are each masters at developing coping mechanisms that allow us to be effective at our jobs and personal lives and to feel safe and powerful. Some of the clients that I have seen go through the biggest shifts did not see themselves as sensitive to others' emotions. They realized the reason they felt this way was due to the amount of energy they were putting into blocking and avoiding other people's emotions. When those emotions did not show up as a threat anymore, the clients were amazed by how much more comfortable they became. This resulted in more confidence and higher levels of energy.

Once we train ourselves to live in this more sovereign state, emotions do not go away. What shifts is that we stop taking on the emotions of others. We are simply left with our own emotions to interact with. Our internal life becomes quite simplified. This will be much clearer to you in chapter seven as we start to experiment with the AL Flow State. You will discover what it feels like as we intentionally entrain with the most aligned part of ourselves. This is the place in us that we fully trust, a place where positivity is readily available and negativity becomes difficult to access.

It is hard to overestimate how big of a role our emotions play in all aspects of our lives. When our emotions get triggered, everything becomes personal. This usually feels extremely disempowering. The moment we enter the rabbit hole of victimhood, we present ourselves in a completely different way, both internally and externally. Our perspective shifts and our insight becomes anything but aligned. We lose our authority and can quickly shift from the role of influencer to influenced. Flow is definitely not accessible from this type of emotional state.

The visualization exercise we are about to do will insulate you from entraining with the emotions of others. It will give you much cleaner access to what you are feeling and wanting. The large majority of my clients find their self-concept stabilize, they become far more positive, and a new sense of confidence quickly follows.

A caveat for two categories of people before we begin. This applies to you: 1) If you are somebody who does not pick up on others emotions, and/or 2) If you have in the past picked up a lot on others' emotions and responded to this overwhelming feeling with the coping mechanism of pulling yourself inward. If either of those descriptions match, you will most likely have to rely on the evidence of change rather than the actual physical sensation of it. Many clients who feel very little physical sensation from the shift know there has been a change by the outcomes rather than feeling the process occur. They start to find themselves being more relaxed, confident, and stable. If you fit into one of those two categories, simply approach this exercise with an open mind. Then be patient and observe yourself and how others respond to you. See if any evidence of change shows up. For those of you that are more tapped into what is going on outside of and around you, this process can create instant, tangible experiences. With this real-time feedback, you will have more incentive to stick with the process. Nothing motivates us like instant results.

What follows is a step-by-step description of the visualization. I recommend you read through the steps and then utilize the free audio recording available at www.insightinfluenceandflow.com to support you through the process. If you have done guided meditations or visualizations in the past, it will be helpful, but don't stress if you haven't. With a little practice, it is something we can all learn to do.

Breaking External Entrainment Visualization (Accessing Sovereignty)

1) Settle yourself into a comfortable space sitting with your back straight.
2) Bring your awareness out to everything around you. Take a moment to see what you feel as you let yourself expand out beyond your body. Put your hands out with your palms open. Visualize the palms of your hands as sensors that are picking up on the emotions of everybody your electromagnetic field comes in contact with. We will refer to this part of your EMF as your emotional body.
3) As you get a sense of what you are picking up on from others, ask your emotional body to rise up and separate from the rest of your EMF.
4) Then close your hands into a fist and visualize all of the sensors in your emotional body shutting down and temporarily turning off.
5) With your hands still closed in a fist, slowly bring them down to your lap. Breathe deeply and feel yourself become relaxed into this more sovereign state of being.

Note: Do not read the next section until after you have completed the visualization exercise with the free audio recording available at www.insightinfluenceandflow.com. What follows contains descriptions of people's experiences with the visualization. I have found that new clients' experiences are generally more profound when they are not going in with an expectation. It is much more powerful to confirm your personal experience by hearing about the experiences of others after the fact rather than going into it with expectations and seeing if your experience matches up.

I have taken hundreds of clients through this exercise with similar results across the board. There are four different categories people tend to fall within. Each person within a category seems to have a similar response to the visualization.

Common Responses to Visualization

1) **I don't pick up on other people's emotions.** We each have our own EMF, as does everybody else on the planet. Our EMFs overlap and influence each other. People in this category were born with or developed the coping mechanism of not focusing in on the influences others' EMFs have on them. This is beneficial from the perspective that they are not pushed around in their conscious mind by others' emotions and don't let their own needs get derailed by over-focusing on the needs of others. The challenge for this category is they tend to be more closed off and less intuitive. If this describes you, your initial experience may have felt like you were simply using your imagination to follow along with the visualization. As I mentioned above, you will most likely have to rely on the evidence of change rather than the actual physical sensation of it. Many clients who feel very little physical sensation from the shift know there has been a change by the outcomes rather than feeling the process occur. They start to find themselves being more relaxed, confident, and stable.

2) **I was always overwhelmed by others' emotions throughout my life, so I have responded by shrinking my EMF and pulling it in as close to my body as possible.** This coping mechanism is a common one. It also comes with some significant challenges. When we pull our EMF in, we shrink our sense of self and the authority we have in

our lives. In a way, we are hiding from the threat of other people's emotions. It is difficult to create powerfully from a place of hiding because the EMF will not be able expand enough to have significant influence on its surroundings. You will most likely have a similar experience to those in the first category with possibly a slight perception of an internal shifting.

3) **I find my ability to feel others' emotions to be a huge strength in my life, and I use it to support everybody.** This is probably the most challenging category. Most of the people this describes are who Dr. Elaine Aron coined the phrase "HSP (Highly Sensitive Person)" for. If you are not familiar with this term, I invite you to check out my web page HSPsolution.com and take the "Am I a Highly Sensitive Person?" quiz. So many people who experience life in this way get their sense of purpose and inner power from their constant drive to help others. This drive comes with some huge challenges. While the intention is to help others, there is also another layer to this category that is generally overlooked. Each big growth we make in our personal development is usually preceded by a period of discomfort, maybe even suffering. I am referring to that period of time when we have outgrown what we have created in our lives or what we have created has reflected back to us in an ugly way. We start to realize that our current circumstances are no longer serving us. This can happen gradually or in many cases quite suddenly. The period between this realization and finding the internal strength to do something about it is a ripe time for suffering.

This suffering serves an important purpose. It is our catalyst for change. It is what makes us say "enough" and find the strength to grow out of it. As an HSP, the moment you pick up on the suffering of others', your instinct is to drop whatever you are doing regardless of how important it is and run to their aid. You are actually feeling their suffering. It shows up in your body almost as if it is happening to you. Relieving their suffering becomes priority one because it is showing up as an actual threat to you. So the first thing you do is help the person to become more comfortable, to quell their suffering. As a result, the person starts to feel more comfortable being stuck. Their desire to change diminishes and they often do not make the big breakthrough they were poised to make. Suffering can serve a powerful purpose. On top of that, the moment the HSP picked up on the other person's suffering, they let go of whatever they were working on in their own life. They became derailed from their own purpose and sacrificed what they were contributing to run to the aid of whoever was in distress.

The illusion is that constantly helping others' out of their suffering is the biggest contribution an HSP can make to the world. This idea is often met with a lot of resistance until the HSP starts to experience a greater degree of sovereignty, and then diminishes even more once they experience moving into the AL Flow State. As the HSP's perspective starts to shift, the next challenge comes in allowing their sense of purpose and personal power to come from a more balanced source. It is empowering to help others because you choose to, rather than out of an uncontrollable, instinctual drive. Over time, my HSP clients learn to balance giving, move out of self-sacrifice, and see the value suffering can play as an agent for change in each of their lives.

People who fall into this category tend to have an awareness of the significant internal shift. Quite often the challenge for these folks is to take some time to experience what this shift creates. It will most likely feel a bit foreign. There is a natural temptation to pull your inner world back to the way you have known it. I encourage you to be patient and observe the inner shifts from a neutral place. When you resist the urge to instantly categorize them as good or bad you receive a much clearer understanding of what you have shifted and how it can serve you.

4) **I find my ability to feel others' emotions to be a gift and a curse. I want to keep the gift so I just deal with the curse.** If this describes you then you are also most likely a HSP. I encourage you to take the quiz on my web page and see what kind of results you get. One advantage you may enjoy is being less attached to the self-sacrifice aspect most HSPs experience. You may engage in this type of response because you feel the need to alleviate the suffering of others that you are likewise experiencing, but you are also clear that this is not necessarily the best course of action. You are in the category that generally makes the smoothest transition into sovereignty and living in the AL Flow State. Be patient and spend some time observing these shifts from a neutral stand point. If you are reading this and fall into one of the other categories, this does not diminish how profound your experience can be as well.

✳✳✳

Now that you have gone through the first visualization, the abstract descriptions I have been giving of sovereignty may start to become more concrete. Sometimes people do need to go through the visualization several times before they really feel and see shifts. Remember that this initial shift is not our end-game. This is just the first step in accessing the AL Flow State.

Each person has their own individual response to the exercise, and at the same time there are similarities that people share across the board. The most common response is a reaction to how quiet it feels when you are not tapped in externally. People often feel powerful in this space at first and then it tends to slowly become more claustrophobic. It can feel very isolating, limited, even sad, and most people report feeling their mental processing slow down. For this reason, I initially end the exercise with participants opening themselves back up externally and returning to their original way of holding their EMF.

In the next chapter, we will repeat this exercise. Then, instead of reopening our emotional bodies externally, we will visualize them opening internally. This creates the meditative state of consciousness that connects us to the AL Flow State. This becomes our access point. If you are having a difficult time wrapping your head around how a simple visualization can really shift your state of consciousness, it is probably a healthy amount of skepticism. I just ask that you hold the possibility open that it really can be this easy and give it a fully committed try.

CHAPTER SEVEN

ACCESSING YOUR ALIGNED LIVING FLOW STATE

Control of consciousness determines the quality of life.
—Mihaly Csikszentmihalyi
Flow: The Psychology of Optimal Experience

For many people, completing the initial "sovereignty" exercise and visualization is a turning point for them. It is often the first glimpse into how powerful these shifts can be. In this chapter, we will take this entrainment to the next level. We will entrain ourselves with a greater sense of self. We will tap into the stability of the earth's electromagnetic field and utilize it to stabilize our own. As I mentioned before, we can expand our visualization of aligning with the pole of the earth to that of aligning with your direct connection with source, God, the divine, or however your religious or spiritual belief system supports you to access that expanded view of self. While for many of you these shifts may feel surreal and magical, we are simply shifting our conscious awareness from the emotional demands of the outside world and entraining them with ourselves.

When people take prescription or recreational drugs they usually aren't surprised when they encounter some sort of a shift in how they are experiencing reality. When we put the substance ibuprofen into our systems, it tells our bodies to decrease the production of hormones that cause inflammation. Then, like magic, our body does what the ibuprofen is asking and pain and inflammation decrease. We have become accustomed to not having direct access to our own bodies control panels. We get a headache, we take a pill, and our headache goes away. This is how we have been taught to interact with our bodies. For most of us, we never even considered that when our bodies are in complete alignment, they can make these shifts on their own, and that we can actually be deliberate about making them happen. We can access our own control panels.

I recognize that opening this conversation is akin to opening Pandora's box. So let me close it again by saying we don't know what is possible until we have new experiences that break old paradigms and open us up to new frontiers. Entering the AL Flow State is a new frontier. There is a reason that most people have only accessed an ultimate flow state through extreme situations and/or mind-altering substances. The intensity of moving into the AL Flow State does feel like something has shifted your consciousness. The beautiful truth is that the "something" is you and your connection to a greater sense of self.

What follows are the steps to accessing the AL Flow State. As in the sovereignty visualization, you will see the best results if you read through the steps first and then utilize the free recording available at www.insightinfluenceandflow.com for your actual visualization.

Accessing Your Aligned Living Flow State

1) Begin with the sovereignty visualization to let go of anything you may be entrained with outside of yourself.

2) Instead of reopening externally, like we did when we finished the original sovereignty exercise, this time we will open internally. With your fists still closed, place one hand over your heart and the other just below your ribcage over the area known as the solar plexus. Visualize your hands representing sensors for your emotional body. As you feel ready, open your hands and use your imagination to "see" each of your emotional body sensors reopening internally.

3) Take a moment to observe your experience. What do you notice? Use this time to bring your awareness into feeling yourself align with your spine. Then ask your consciousness to show you the alignment of the EMF of the earth. Ask to become aware of the energy of the earth's EMF starting to run in through the top of your head. Visualize and feel this energy running all the way down your spine and out your tailbone into the earth, right down through the pole of the earth. As you "see" the energy move completely through the earth, invite this same energy to run back up through your spine and out the top of your head letting it follow the alignment of the earth's EMF. Become aware of your own EMF aligning and becoming entrained with that of the earth's.

4) We will now utilize this energy to charge our body and entire EMF. Move your attention to your heart. (Not your literal heart, but where your heart lines up with your spine in the center of your body.) We will invite this flow of energy to come in through the heart and fill this whole

area around your heart, chest, shoulders, spine, back, and shoulder blades. Invite the energy to move out your arms, to your elbows, then forearms, wrists, hands, and fingers. As you get a sense of fullness through this whole area of your body invite this energy to come up from the earth and through your tailbone and spine to fill this same entire area around your heart. If at any point throughout this visualization you feel like the energy is getting stuck and not flowing through you, simply move your attention to the top of your head and watch the energy flow in. Then move your attention to the base of your spine and watch the energy flow in. It should be like filling a bathtub. You just turn on the tap and watch it fill. I find that once you reconnect with the flow, the energy will start to move again where it had felt blocked. As you feel this step complete, give permission for this energy to start to radiate out from you. Stay centered in your body and sovereignty as you send your EMF radiating out from your body. Visualize this radiating energy becoming a big sphere of light and sharing this powerful aligned energy with everybody and everything around you. Be very intentional in not following this energy so you remain internal rather than starting to re-entrain with the external.

5) Move your focus down your spine to your solar plexus (the area just below your rib cage aligned with your spine). Repeat the same steps of inviting this energy through the top of your head, and give it permission to fill all through your ribs. Then invite the energy to flow up through the tailbone filling this same space. Once you get a sense that your solar plexus has filled with this energy, give it permission to join the sphere of light around your heart. Let the energy start to radiate out, as you stay centered in it.

6) Move your focus further down your spine to just below your naval. This area is known as the sacral region. Repeat the steps of filling your sacral region and all your internal organs with this energy, coming in through the top of your head and then up through the base of the spine. Invite the sphere of light around the heart and solar plexus to expand to include your sacral and radiate out from your body while you stay aligned and centered in it.

7) Move your attention further down your spine to your root (the area at the base of your spine). Repeat the steps above including running the energy down your legs and out the base of your spine, filling your own center channel or "pole" that aligns with the earth's, allowing the energy flowing down your spine to become one with the energy flowing through the pole of the earth.

8) Move your attention to your throat and repeat these same steps.

9) Move your attention to your head now and repeat these same steps. Quite often people feel a sense of moving from the front of the brain to feeling much more relaxed and at ease as they slide to the back of the brain and spinal column. This is the point where the sense of moving into the AL Flow State most often starts to become apparent.

10) Move your attention to the very top of your head to the space known as your crown. Repeat the same steps and feel the energy continue above your head, tying in with the pole of the earth's EMF.

11) In the final step we will become aware of the toroidal field that our EMF creates, just like the earth's. Visualize your EMF gathering at the top of your crown, running down your spine, out the base of your tailbone, and then flowing around the outside of you and back through your

crown. This continuous flow is the natural formation all EMFs take. Most people feel a sense of their energy instantly feeling less chaotic and more organized.

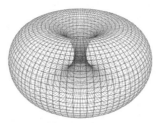

12) Connect with you spinal column, bringing your focus to the place where your brain and spine connect. Feel the energy flow through this space. Follow it down the spine and connect with the tailbone. Use the brain stem, spine, and tailbone as your internal reference points. We can use them to replace the external reference points we would use to get our bearings. As we entrain with these internal reference points, we are no longer externally influenced in the same way.

CHAPTER EIGHT

PLAYING WITH BEING IN AND OUT OF ALIGNMENT

Life naturally reorganizes itself when we are true to our-selves and everything can fall into its right place. That's when "the highest good of all" naturally happens.

—Maria Erving
Facebook, March 28, 2018

O nce I take a client into the AL Flow State, I always have them experiment with how differently they experience frustra-tions and drama from this place. I recommend you try this experiment as well. It demonstrates how powerful a shift moving into your alignment really is. Before you begin, identify some-thing in your life that has been frustrating for you. People often choose challenging relationships or the way something is playing out at work or in their home/social lives that they wish was dif-ferent. Don't go into your "story," just allow the idea to be present. Take a minute to get in touch with the electromagnetic energy running in through the top of your head and out your spine. Pay particular attention to visualizing the energy running through your brain stem where your brain and spine connect. For many people, this quickly becomes a tangible experience. Now that you know you are in your alignment, see what shows up for you as you observe the frustration you picked out. It is important that you don't go into any ideas you have already come up with, but rather just observe the situation. What do you notice?

Now physically move your head over by leaning to the left or right about a foot and check in again with your frustrating experience. How does it feel from here? Then bring yourself back into alignment and get in touch with the flow of electromagnetic energy running through you again. Now what do you notice? I will talk about what people commonly experience with this as well as why in the next section.

Please note, as with the sovereignty visualization, do not read the next section until after you have completed the A.L. Flow State visualization exercise with the audio recording. What follows contains descriptions of people's experiences with the visualization. I have found that new clients' experiences are generally more profound when they are not going in with any expectations. It is much more powerful to confirm your personal experience by hearing about the experiences of others after the fact than going into it with expectations and seeing if your experience matches up. Now that you have had your own experience, here are some of the most common responses I hear back from my clients:

-The moment I visualized my emotional body sensors opening up internally, I had this overwhelming sense of coming home.
-I felt such peace and ease, like everything is okay.
-I couldn't seem to access my worry and anger.
-Everything felt quiet and still, almost like I was meditating but I could still function in the world.

-I instantly became clear about what I wanted and how I was feeling.

-I did not feel the same push to take action. I instantly became more patient and precise with my actions. In the past, I would just start pushing to change things externally because I was uncomfortable internally.

-I could feel emotions but they no longer felt threatening, they were more like information, rather than overwhelming and derailing. I felt more logical and in control.

When playing with being in and out of alignment clients usually have similar experiences as well. They have a tough time accessing drama or frustration when they are aligned. They tend to feel less connected to frustration, more stable in their experience, and lose the feeling that "this is personal." As soon as the client leans to the side, physically moving their head over, it breaks their entrainment with their own and the earth's EMF. They start to entrain with the frustration instead and move right into a negative emotional response. The drama becomes readily available again, and their body starts to feel less comfortable. The moment they move back into alignment and begin re-entraining with their EMF, they regain the positive experience.

So many people are addicted to their drama. This can be a huge challenge in learning to maintain the AL Flow State. If drama and frustration are where your mind naturally goes, this will be a habit you will need to break. Being in flow and being in drama are mutually exclusive states of mind. You can't be in both places at the same time. I observe the majority of my clients experiencing a bit of discomfort in not being able to access the negative emotions they had become used to being in at all times. They will enter their flow state, and then as we talk, I will observe them slowly move their heads forward or sideways. The clarity and feeling of being uplifted is foreign to most people and therefore can be initially uncomfortable. When I ask clients why they are sitting with their heads cocked sideways or careening forward, they always respond with, "I don't know, it just feels more comfortable." What they really mean is that it feels more familiar. We aren't doing this work to create familiar, or to create more of the same. We are doing this work to move beyond old limitations and patterns. We are creating a whole new way of being, a new operating system. Of course for most people this starts out feeling unfamiliar and slightly uncomfortable.

On the other hand, at this point a portion of our clients experience amnesia-like symptoms. For those clients, this new alignment feels so natural and familiar that they seem to almost instantly forget their old way of being. It is rather bizarre to watch these clients talk about their current experience as if it has always been present. I have clients record their sessions and have heard from several of them how shocking it is hearing themselves before they moved into alignment. The old limitations and dramas seem laughable to them as they hear themselves talking about challenges that only existed in their minds.

As humans we have many predictable patterns and paradigms that we have been trained to believe through our experiences. We reflect experiences of limitations and struggle back and forth between each other, each reflection reconfirming the previous one. These experiences create a concrete shared reality. Through this process of claiming our sovereignty, entraining with ourselves and the EMF of the earth, and moving into the AL Flow State, we leave that old, agreed upon reality behind. We have an instant expansion and paradigm shift as we begin operating outside of the old illusions. Congratulations, you are experiencing the balancing point between ordinary reality and non-ordinary reality. You have accessed the ultimate estuary of consciousness, the AL Flow State.

CHAPTER NINE

FLOW INDUCING ENVIRONMENTS

That's been one of my mantras—focus and simplicity. Simple can be harder than complex: You have to work hard to get your thinking clean to make it simple. But it's worth it in the end because once you get there, you can move mountains.

—Steve Jobs
Interview with *Wired*, 1996

D r. Mihaly Csikszentmihalyi, author of *Flow* and the person who literally coined the term "flow" identified four ideal conditions for being in flow. Dr. Keith Sawyer author of *Group Genius*, who studied under Csikszentmihalyi at the University of Chicago expanded on his work by identifying ten ideal social conditions for entering flow. The idea is that the more of these conditions that are present, the easier it is for us to access flow. While the Aligned Living techniques we have been using can allow us to work outside of external factors, Csikszentmihalyi's and Sawyer's ideal flow conditions undoubtedly support our process.

Up until this point, we have been operating in sovereignty. We have been achieving flow regardless of the situation or circumstances. I share Csikszentmihalyi's and Sawyer's ideal flow conditions here to enhance what you are already creating. Let's take a look at these ideal conditions and see how they apply.

The first and most important of Csikszentmihalyi's ideal conditions is having the right amount of challenge in relation to skill. If the task is too easy we tend to lose focus and if the task is too difficult we may move into frustration or overwhelm. As you can imagine neither mundane or overwhelming tasks or situations are ideal for being in flow. This slight step outside of your comfort zone helps you keep your focus in the present moment. His second ideal condition is having a clear goal. This gives you the "what" to focus on and provides you with the certainty to maintain your focus. Csikszentmihalyi's third ideal condition is the presence of immediate feedback. The more immediate feedback we get the more our focus remains in the present moment ready to adjust and course correct. Csikszentmihalyi found this to be particularly true in relation to knowing how close you are to completing the clear goal (the second ideal condition) Csikszentmihalyi's fourth ideal condition is the freedom to fully concentrate on the task. When we have uninterrupted time and space to focus on a singular task flow is a much more likely outcome. [8]

Expanding on Csikszentmihalyi's research, Sawyer has brought us great insight into group flow and what he calls "The Ten Conditions for Group Flow." What follows are Sawyer's titles for "The Ten Conditions for Group Flow" and descriptions that I have condensed into my own words as an overview of his concepts. [9]

---

8 Csikszentmihalyi, Dr. Mihaly. 1990. *Flow: The Psychology of Optimal Experience*. NewYork: HarperCollins Publishers.
9 Sawyer, Dr. Keith. 2008. *Group Genius: The Creative Power of Collaboration*. New York: Basic Books.

1. "The group's goal" This puts the team on the same page. It has them working towards the same goal, which creates an accountability to the group and helps maintain an awareness of how close they are to achieving the group's goal. It is also important that each member has an opportunity to bring their own expertise and creativity without having too much latitude to stray from the cohesiveness of the group.

2. "Close listening" When group members can listen closely with their full attention on what is being shared rather than the members focusing on what they want to say next, flow is increased. It is also important to find the balance of innovative ideas without shutting other people down.

3. "Complete concentration" The more the group situation requires you to be aware of your role and that of others, the more likely it is to sharpen your focus. Interestingly, stressful deadlines can diminish flow as members are likely to be distracted from the task at hand by the squeeze of time pressures.

4. "Being in control" It's important for each member to feel a combination of autonomy and competency in group flow. When they feel a freedom in choosing what they work on and feel they have the skills to complete the task while still allowing the commitment to the team to be the priority, flow is easier to access.

5. "Blending egos" Group members need to be able to let go of their focus on their individual selves and submerse themselves into the collaboration, allowing ideas to build on each other without thought to who is generating them.

6. "Equal participation" When each member feels they and their colleagues are each contributing similar value, flow is much more readily available. If there is a person in the role of manager it is important that they do not try to

dominate or put their ideas over others. Micromanaging, even at subtle levels kills flow.

7. "Familiarity" The entire team must be familiar with each other and already have developed effective and positive spoken and unspoken communication. This allows the team to keep moving forward without losing momentum due to the need for lengthy explanations. It is important for the members to be familiar with each other but not so much that a complacency shows up. Remember, being slightly outside of your comfort zone supports flow.

8. "Communication" A group flow is assisted by a constant feedback loop of communication that is focused on forward movement. The entire group must listen attentively to each other's ideas and build on them without alienating any of the members.

9. "Keeping it moving forward" This is not about following ideas good or bad, it is about contributing rather than shutting ideas down. The group can then move forward building on each other's ideas. The additive nature creates momentum, togetherness, and innovation.

10. "The potential for failure" Having some degree of physical, mental, or creative risk present raises the stakes and ups everybody's involvement and commitment.

Take some time and experiment with these ideal conditions. See how you can deliberately put them in place to help you move deeper into the AL Flow State and—just as importantly—maintain it. Remember my words of caution, however, and continue in the sovereignty that has allowed you to achieve flow regardless of your situation or circumstances. These ideal conditions are not prerequisites to flow when we use the Aligned Living techniques to access it, but rather are supportive of the process.

CHAPTER TEN

WHAT IF THIS ISN'T WORKING FOR ME?

When you knock on the door of opportunity do not be surprised that it is work who will answer.

—Brendon Burchard
Tweet 12:27 PM – 1 May 2016

The vast majority of you will read this chapter title and think, "Are you kidding me? Everything feels different." But some of you will get stuck. The most common challenge people have with the Aligned Living work is fittingly paradoxical in nature. First, our mind thinks the work is too simple to create the kinds of changes we experience, and second, the changes are too intense for some people to step into all at once. They think, "I'm not doing enough, and things are changing too much." Interestingly, when we are in the AL Flow State we don't feel this way. We can only access this limited thinking by reconnecting with our old level of consciousness. I have found the easiest way to approach this shift is to see it as a game and move into a place of discovery and exploration.

Often people who are finding the shifts that come with staying aligned challenging to continuously engage in have a tendency to take themselves fairly seriously. They are afraid of looking like a fool and diving into something that is not real. They want the growth and changes others are experiencing, but at some level they are holding back. They are preserving their skepticism and composure in case this is an elaborate hoax. Other people got duped, but not them. Essentially, they are being reserved and only giving the work a half-hearted try.

I was in college in the nineties when Magic Eye posters had just come out. For the image to work, you had to stare at it and keep your eyes from focusing. You would gaze at the poster, and then all of a sudden your vision would pop into this 3-D world like magic. For most people this doesn't happen instantly. You have to sit there like an idiot, staring but not staring, waiting for something extraordinary to happen.

At the time, these posters had not yet made it to the small upstate New York town where I was attending college, so we had never heard of them. A buddy of mine had just returned from a road trip to Florida and brought one back for us to experience for the first time. This guy also loved to play practical jokes on everybody. There were about seven of us sitting around staring at the poster and, one by one, we had the 3-D experience. As each of us would have our breakthrough, we would freak out about how cool it was. Eventually all but two of us had been able to see what a moment before had seemed impossible.

The two guys who hadn't been able to were twin brothers who were often on the receiving end of our practical jokes. They became convinced that this was exactly what was happening with the poster. They decided that the rest of us were faking having an outrageous experience to trick them into staring at this damn poster like fools. They were sure this was another elaborate joke aimed at them. We left the poster in our living room throughout the week. When nobody was around, the brothers would secretly stare at the poster, trying to have an experience. They couldn't give it their all at first, otherwise they risked being fools. But by the end of the week, they were able to see the incredible 3-D image. It took them a lot longer, not because they were skeptical, but because they didn't give it a full try. Please, maintain your skepticism, but put the fear of being a fool to the side long enough to go all in. You can even keep your game to yourself if it makes you feel more comfortable.

Another key component to the Aligned Living process working is allowing yourself to float in a rather pliable state as you transition into the AL Flow State. Some people are highly aware of their baseline internal state of consciousness. The moment they feel it move, there is a natural tendency for them to refocus back into their old baseline. This is actually quite similar to the experience of the Magic Eye 3-D pictures. With these pictures you have to allow your vision to move out of focus and float in this pliable state in order to refocus in the new experience of the image becoming three-dimensional. If you try to intentionally refocus your vision you simply pop back to your old baseline. I have seen clients block themselves from entering the AL Flow State in this same way. Relax and trust the process. Allow the experience to be like a game.

Sometimes people's struggle with this work is about timing. They are not in a place in their lives right now to begin doing this work, and that's fine. We all have times we feel more secure and ready to take on challenges and times we get more easily overwhelmed. I am hesitant to add this here because if this were true you probably would have discounted this book much earlier on. Just in case you are pushing yourself out of commitment to seeing it through, I decided to include the next story. You may even be pushing yourself to continue reading to prove something to a friend that recommended the book. Sometimes people go through the motions and say, "There, I tried it and nothing happened." Maybe you are making yourself do this for a relationship. Your partner did this work and wants you to join them in their new world. Possibly you want to go through the process to prove it wrong. Whatever your motivation is, if it is not an internal drive to grow and develop yourself, then the beneficial shifts will be much harder to come by.

I had a new client schedule a session with me. She was referred by a friend who had created powerful shifts in her life from our work together. The moment this client showed up, I could feel her fear and defensiveness. In hindsight, I should have just told her that flow work was not a great match for her right now and stopped the session before it even got started. Unfortunately, I went ahead despite my intuition setting off alarms in my head. It is seldom that clients are not a good fit. When this is the case, however, they are almost always referred by a friend that wants me to "fix them." I have finally learned to watch for this over the years of fine-tuning my coaching practice.

As I mentioned earlier, I generally encourage people to record our sessions so they can go back and relisten to them. The information we cover is a lot to take in during one sitting and the recording also provides them with a personalized visualization meditation to use. This client was quite hesitant to record, but once I explained why people appreciate having the recording, she suspiciously agreed. We began her session talking about what was going on for her and, more importantly, what her role in it was. Then about fifteen minutes into the session, she suddenly stopped her recording and erased it, saying, "I would never listen to this again, and I sure wouldn't want anybody else to." She was feeling exposed and defensive. Her whole mindset was on keeping her challenges hidden, not overcoming them. Her ego had been working overtime blaming everybody and everything in her life for how miserable she was. Her ego was so successful at this that she claimed to be very happy despite the fact that she was surrounded by "morons." I was hoping that once we did the visualization work and moved into the AL Flow State this would shift for her. She sat there appearing to quietly play along as we moved into the sovereignty visualization and then into the AL Flow. She showed little external response as she had each experience. We ended her ninety-minute session, and she left.

The next day she reviewed me on Yelp. She was adamant that I was a fraud and nobody should come to me for anything. She wrote that I was babbling about things that had nothing to do with her and that I did some weird meditation for a couple of minutes. She claimed our session was about a half hour, but I charged her for an hour and a half. Apparently, she had shut down once we did the meditation. Our minds are powerful. She was so committed to staying stuck in her safe, yet miserable world that she had blocked out most of the experience. Her response was definitely the most extreme I have seen, but it does illustrate the role our internal resistance can play.

If you are finding yourself becoming resistant to this work to the point where you are avoiding what is showing up, this is most likely relevant to you. It is time to decide if you want to commit to growth right now or not. For some people, we are simply planting a seed for what is possible. Maybe you are not feeling empowered enough at this moment to nurse that seed into a powerful shift in your life. I have seen many clients come back after spending time in their old suffering and frustrating limitations. Once they know there is another possibility out there, they eventually want to come back and reexplore it. This is usually triggered by negative life experiences repeating until their desire for change outweighs their fear of change.

The reactions they get from the people in their lives is another common way clients get derailed from flow work. When we are in the AL Flow State, we are received quite differently.

As previously discussed, our EMF is very different and so are our instincts of what to say and how to act. Every relationship has preexisting understandings of how each person will present themselves. By moving into the AL Flow State, we are breaking those old agreements. It is not uncommon for the people in our lives who have built their foundations in connection with ours to get concerned when we start changing. It forces them to change, too, and this is not always what they want. Since you are the one initiating the change, it can make them feel out of control. It can feel like you are inflicting this change on them, either through abandonment or by having new expectations.

It can be difficult for the people in our lives to understand what we are doing, and it can feel threatening. Of course they feel this way. It should be expected. You will need to decide how much you can share about the process with them. The more they know about what you are doing, the more opportunity they have to understand it. Keep in mind, not everybody is ready to understand the changes you are creating and this can be very emotionally triggering. It is up to you to feel out how much is appropriate to share with each individual. There are a variety of ways these triggers are activated, showing us so much about the basis of the relationships. I will break this down into three categories: energy vampires, competitors, and partners.

Energy vampires have been feeding off our energy field. They have been knowingly or unknowingly taking advantage of the fact that we have been living externally. Once we start to entrain internally, our energy is no longer available to them. At this point, they often reach out to us and complain about feeling tired and unmotivated. This is ironic because this is how you probably felt around them when you were externally entrained. Energy vampires are not necessarily bad people, but they tend to be dependent on others in many ways. They feel recharged by being around the people they feel connected to. Once we learn to spot energy vampires, we realize they are everywhere. This gives us another reason to commit to staying in the AL Flow State, and can partially explain the increase in vitality and energy we feel while aligned.

Competitors are our friends and colleagues that have appeared to be working with us but once we start to grow feel threatened and diminished by our success. I have had many clients tell me about how people they had viewed as friends and colleagues reached out and in some way attempted to take the wind out of their sails. More often than not, this would be some form of projection. "You haven't been yourself lately. You seem like you are struggling with …" fill in the blank with whatever topic or emotion the person is feeling left behind about. Of course, if a trusted friend or colleague brings a concern to you, don't just automatically discount it. Take the time to bring their concern into your alignment and see how it holds up. In the next chapter, you will learn a technique I call "Aligned Perspectives." This will provide a perfect opportunity to try this out.

Our third category, partners, are the people in our lives that are more likely to experience our growth as some sort of abandonment. They have been accustomed to our support and the ways we may have enabled them by being emotionally codependent in their lives. The moment we become sovereign, they feel the shift and can easily take it personally. Our EMFs stop connecting in the same way they used to, and our partners can feel it and usually misinterpret it. Their interpretation is usually fear based. A young female client of mine in her mid-twenties shared with me how her live-in boyfriend responded to her shift. She had told him that she met with me that morning but had not described exactly what we were working on or how she may feel different to him. They spent the rest of the day together, and then later in the evening he came up to her with a distraught look on his face and asked, "Are we breaking up?" She broke out laughing and explained what was going on. Of course this sounded quite outrageous to him, but eventually he trusted and then embraced her new independence and confidence.

I can't stress enough how important it is to explain to those closest to us, at whatever level they can understand, what we are doing and how it may come across. I often share that story with new clients to drive the point home. It is hard for people to imagine they will be received so differently until they experience the reactions of the people they regularly interact with. It can be tempting to think you are doing something wrong if the people around you become unhappy, but really those people just need to adjust to the changing you. Most clients experience some resistance to these changes. The more you can prepare people and support them through this transition period, the smoother it will go. Once you experience the "coming home" feeling of moving into the AL Flow State, you won't want to give it up. Being aligned feels like being true to yourself. If you deny yourself this to make others more comfortable, resentment will most likely build, creating a problem of its own. The cleanest and most appropriate way to handle this shift is to be true to yourself, communicate well with those closest to you, and support them without taking on responsibility for regulating their emotional states.

CHAPTER ELEVEN
INSIGHT AND INNOVATION

To raise new questions, new possibilities, to regard old problems from a new angle, requires creative imagination and marks real advance in science.

—Albert Einstein
Albert Einstein and Leopold Infield,
The Evolution of Physics

A shift in perspective is the first thing most clients report as they move into AL Flow State. In this chapter, we will be more intentional in identifying this shift and what it can open up for us. We will start operating outside of the limitations of many of our old fears and triggers and feel comfortable allowing our minds to stray beyond their normal boundaries. With this shift, we enter the realm of innovative thinking.

When I train Aligned Living coaches, I sit in on a couple of their initial sessions. One of the coaches in training, Marty, was taking one of her first clients through the alignment process. Her client, an entrepreneur named Sherry, had come in looking for clarity. She was planning the launch of a new business, developing an idea she had been formulating for some time. Sherry had already talked with multiple friends and colleagues about her plans, and everybody had given her positive feedback, told her what a great idea she had, and how well it fit her. The more people she talked to, the more the idea became concrete. Sherry was very good at identifying potential pitfalls—so good, in fact, that she kept getting stuck focusing on the challenges she needed to overcome to move forward. She was struggling to create any forward momentum because of all the roadblocks she knew she had to solve.

Once Marty had taken Sherry through the first part of her session and alignment, she took her through the Aligned Perspective technique. This exercise opens your perspective and creates a fertile environment for innovative thinking. The process, which I will explain step-by-step below, begins by accessing the AL Flow State. The key to this technique working is staying aligned throughout the whole process. We use the Aligned Perspective technique in just about any situation where we want greater clarity or to move beyond limiting paradigms.

The old way of thinking and processing was to use our imagination to simulate or recreate the experience. We would essentially travel with our minds into the experience. Many of us would even feel the experience as our emotions and triggers would play out. Our bodies would not necessarily know the difference between what we were creating with our imaginations and the real experience. These emotions would move our perspective all over the place. In victory we would feel huge and powerful, in defeat we would shrink and struggle, and in confusion we would flounder. We would seldom have breakthroughs because we would be investigating the experience from inside it, trapped in the emotional limitations that helped create the problem in the first place. Albert Einstein famously said, "No problem can be solved from the same level of consciousness that created it." Each of us have had a long history of attempting just that.

Instead of imagining the situation and leaving our center to examine it, now we maintain our alignment and invite the situation to come to us. We utilize our imagination to bring the experience into our aligned and centered space. From this place, our perspectives are not being pushed around by the different emotions we are feeling—we are maintaining our highest sustainable perspective. We entrain with our own EMF instead of the experience we are processing. We are even, balanced, and grounded. This gives us a new perspective and level of consciousness where we can see what really matches us. Even when you imagined yourself in victory, you were most likely not in a balanced state, but rather experiencing the high of victory. While this is an enjoyable experience, it is most likely not the clearest place to create from. From the altered state this high provides, we tend to overestimate our ability and future success. It is a wonderful place to celebrate in, but it is not sustainable. That "I'm on top of the world!" elated state is perfect in that moment but obviously not the place to launch or plan from.

As Sherry invited her business idea to come join her in her aligned state, it looked completely different to her. She described seeing what was important about the idea, why she was doing it. She saw the parts she had added on from other people's feedback and realized those additions were where many of the roadblocks were showing up. With the precision of a surgeon with a scalpel, she cut away the extras that were bogging down the idea. She discovered her entrance point to access clients and the steps to initiate her project. In a matter of minutes, she moved from feeling stuck to empowered, from confusion to clarity. The three of us sat there laughing at the ease and simplicity of the process and Sherry's breakthroughs.

Living in the AL Flow State naturally makes us more decisive. The more we intentionally utilize the Aligned Perspectives technique, the more we find ourselves developing the habit of examining and feeling situations from within our alignment. This habit creates a decisiveness that happens in that "black box" realm that I introduced in chapter three. We feel so clear in what matches us and what does not. The instant disharmony or resonance we feel allows us to pursue potential possibilities without getting sidetracked by distractions. This decisiveness is now commonly becoming a highly sought after trait in modern business leaders.

I have witnessed these types of breakthroughs over and over again with different clients. I have also witnessed what all too often follows this clarity. Maintaining the AL Flow State is a big commitment. Unless you are in that small percentage who enter flow and never look back, you are going to have to work at the process to maintain the results. This is precisely why I created the Aligned Living coaching program—to support and guide people as they learn to live in the AL Flow. Of course you can be successful at this work by yourself, too, and if you are somebody who can make a daily commitment and stick with it, this book will give you all the tools you need to begin the process.

Sherry had left her session with incredible clarity and the tools to make Aligned Living a sustained state. Three weeks later Sherry checked back in with Marty and came in for another session. She had done some traveling and connecting with different people, and throughout the process had slowly slid back into her old consciousness. Within minutes, Marty assisted Sherry back into her aligned state of the AL Flow. The clarity and direction was once more available to Sherry. Many of the clients we work with go through a similar experience. These tools seem so simple that it is hard for our mind to grasp how much changes when we use them. It really is not logical at first. Until clients accept how impactful this work is, they generally need to go back and forth between their old consciousness and the AL Flow State several times. Until we recognize the true value of something, it is hard to put our full commitment into it. This is no different.

Aligned Perspective Technique

1) Enter the AL Flow State.
2) Pick the topics or people you want to check in on.
3) Get in touch with the flow of electromagnetic energy coming through your body. Bring your focus to how it feels as it runs through your brain and brain stem. Feel yourself moving to the back of the brain as you allow yourself to relax into this flow.
4) Use your imagination to invite the person or situation into your energy field. Stay entrained with your own electromagnetic field as the person or situation shows up. Be careful not to go into what you feel you already know, or the story you have already formed. Just observe, like you are watching a movie and have no idea what is going to happen. Don't even speculate, just see what shows up.
5) How does the person or situation appear to you? Does it seem smaller or bigger than you thought? Does it feel in or out of resonance to you? What do you notice that is different from your existing story? At this stage, the clarity usually comes in quickly.

CHAPTER TWELVE

ACCESSING YOUR INTUITION

Sometimes a dream almost whispers... It never shouts.
Very hard to hear. So you have to, every day of your lives,
be ready to hear what whispers in your ear.

—Steven Spielberg
From Academy Awards speech

Intuition has slowly become an acceptable concept in the mainstream. We now hear many business leaders talking openly about their "gut instincts," having a "feeling," or sometimes simply using the word "intuition." There is no doubt that intuition plays a role in every decision we make. The more we own that truth, the more we can utilize our intuition. We tend to act as if it is our intuition's job to get our attention, but quite the opposite is true. As Steven Spielberg describes, it is like a whisper, and we need to be ready to hear it. We need to be tuned in to it—in other words, entrained with our own intuition. When we are in the AL Flow State, we experience a quietness that makes the whisper of our intuition seem louder and more accessible. This is related to, yet goes far beyond, the decisiveness we feel while being in resonance or out of resonance with people, ideas, and opportunities. Our intuition brings us new ideas and inspiration. It helps guide us through our lives. This can be a tricky and confusing path full of traps and opportunities. Living in the AL Flow State gives you access to your intuition, but learning how to have it support you is a skill that can only be developed through experience. This chapter is dedicated to fast-tracking this learning curve. Over the years, I have experienced and learned to navigate through the challenges of being intuitive. The following lessons, which I often learned the hard way, can assist you in having your intuition support you without fooling you into misinterpreting the "whisper."

The first thing to get clear on is recognizing the difference between an emotional, egoic reaction and your intuition. I believe using the terms "gut feeling" or "gut instinct" to describe our intuition has increased this confusion. I was recently in a business training where we were talking about intuition and the role it plays in our decisions. A woman was sharing about how whenever she follows her intuition it seems to steer her down the wrong path. She gave an account of experiences where she hired employees based on her gut instinct. She got a warm feeling in her body while interviewing them. She hired them but, as much as she liked them, they proved to be terrible fits for the job. What this hiring manager was experiencing was a positive emotional response to the applicant and their EMF. If she were interviewing potential friends, this may have served her well. Unfortunately that was not the case. (Of course, our emotions can be misleading with friendships as well and guide us into repeating old patterns.) She had also described negative responses to applicants that she chose not to hire. She was clearly operating in the realm of emotion rather than intuition.

Once you understand the differences, it is easy to tell which it is you are experiencing. An emotional egoic reaction or response is a physical and emotional feeling. It is triggered by past experience, whether positive or negative, and takes you into emotional states that reflect those prior experiences. When we realize what we are experiencing, we can see how misdirecting and confusing emotional reactions can be. The new CFO that you hired because interacting with her gave you a warm fuzzy feeling (unconsciously generated by her similarities to your childhood babysitter), will most likely not be the right fit. On the opposite end, you may have overlooked the best candidate because of an emotional gut reaction to a shared mannerism they have with an old teacher you couldn't stand. While it is logical that we have emotional reactions, the reactions themselves are seldom logical and will often steer us in the wrong direction.

Our intuition is quite different. In fact, when we are emotionally triggered it is near impossible to hear "the whisper" of our intuition. Emotions speak much louder, and if we let them, they will dominate the conversations in our head. Much like the overbearing coworker trying to force people to agree with his or her opinion by loudly dominating the conversation, our emotions can run us over. The only way to hear our intuition is to quiet our emotions. Our intuition can also have a physical element or "gut feeling," but it is seldom overwhelming. When we move into the AL Flow State, we quiet our emotions and create the opportunity for our intuition to be heard.

This too can be tricky to navigate. Sometimes our intuition is just presenting opportunities for growth. There is this false idea that says, "If I listen to my intuition, life will be easier." Whenever we set an intention to achieve something in our lives, we either step into it or are confronted by obstacles within ourselves that are blocking that manifestation. Our intuition actually follows a logical path in assisting us in overcoming those obstacles. If you had a dream of being a high-level executive for a particular corporation (for this example, we will call it the OmegAlignment Corporation), you would find out what was required to achieve that goal. Your research might reveal that the company hires its top executives from within and they don't consider employees to be qualified unless they have their MBA. Let's say you don't work for the company yet and you don't have an MBA. If you are seriously committed to your goal, the next steps are obvious. Acquire a job with the OmegAlignment Corporation at your current qualification level, and start your MBA. Those are the first two obstacles between you and your goal, so they must be solved first. You can't just give the CEO a call and let her know you are her new executive and will be starting on Monday.

Our intuition works in a similar way. Let's say Jenny has the same goal of being a high-level executive with the OmegAlignment Corporation. She already works for them and has her MBA. Now the obstacles are a bit less obvious. Once she commits to her goal, though, her intuition starts working on her behalf. In this scenario, we will say her obstacle is in her belief system. Jenny is somebody who self-isolates when she is upset. Her supervisor notices this and labels her as "not a team player." Jenny is caught up in her own story and has no idea any of this is happening or even keeping her from advancing and achieving her goal. This is where her intuition comes in.

Jenny's corporation is restructuring and her whole department is being reassigned to different teams. Jenny gets a strong intuitive hit that she should be on Gregory's team. Gregory is a new middle-level manager with the company. He was brought in as part of the restructuring process. Gregory is a complete unknown, but Jenny trusts her intuition. She makes her wishes known and is delighted to find out she is on Gregory's team. On day one, Jenny's old patterns show up in her new situation. The smiling Gregory that she saw in the elevator on his way to his initial interview is not the Gregory that showed up as her boss. As Jenny begins feeling overwhelmed by all the newness, she unconsciously starts withdrawing from the group. Gregory immediately calls her out in front of everybody: "Jenny, on my team we all work together. Nobody is better than anybody else." Jenny is in complete shock, having no idea why he would have gotten the impression she thought she was better than anyone else. For the next two weeks, Jenny feels attacked by Gregory at every turn. She wants to leave the company and can't believe she had the intuitive hit to have him as a boss. "How could I have been so wrong?" she wonders. Jenny has completely abandoned her original goal of being a high-level executive. The worst part is that the rest of her team seems to like this jerk she has as a boss. When Jenny returns from lunch on Friday, a notice pops up on her calendar—she has a meeting with Gregory at 4:00 p.m. It is also cc'd to Angie from HR. Panic instantly sets in.

At 4:00 pm Jenny walks into Gregory's office and sees Angie is already there. Gregory explains he invited Angie so their meeting can be documented. He goes on to explain the behavior he has seen from Jenny and her coworkers response to her. In that moment, she realizes how her self-isolation is being received. Not only that, how it has often been received in the past. The past two weeks of suffering that her intuition had guided her into is potentially about to pay off.

Where the story goes from here is completely up to Jenny's relationship with her ego and her willingness to grow. She could just as easily push back against Gregory and raise the stakes of the lesson her intuition guided her into. She could lose her job and move into victimhood. On the other hand, she could own her realization and make the changes necessary to stop self-isolating. She could let this be the catalyst to reach out for help with her anxiety and feelings of being overwhelmed. This could be the turning point that puts her on track toward being a high-level executive. Our intuition guides us into whatever growth opportunities we need. They are seldom "easy," but they do support us if we let them.

As I worked with my intuition, like Jenny, I have received many "hits" of what to do. About 90 percent of these hits have guided me to run full speed into the brick walls of life that swiftly taught me what I needed to learn and grow. As difficult as many of those experiences were, now that I am able to see their purpose, I am glad I had them. However, the next bit of wisdom I am about to share certainly would have come in handy if I had known about it a long time ago. Although many of our intuitive hits are guiding us into growth opportunities, running full speed into the brick wall or ignoring our intuition are not the only options. When we are maintaining the AL Flow State, we can bring our intuitive "hits" into our alignment with us. Then we can ask our intuitive self two very simple questions. "What am I being set up to learn from this experience?" and "Can I learn it by processing the potential experience in theory, or do I need to live it?" Asking those two questions before taking any bold intuitively guided action has brought much peace and grounding back into my life. Sometimes we do need to actually run into that brick wall, and other times we can learn the lesson from the comfort of our own inner world.

Your intuition is completely here to support you. It is like a teacher assisting you in your growth. It can only help you create what you are ready to step into. When you ask your intuition to guide you into something you are not yet ready to achieve, then it guides you into the growth opportunities necessary to become ready. The teachers that let us get away with not bringing our best may have been our favorites in the moment, but the teachers that pushed us into our greatness are the ones we feel the most gratitude for. You can count on your intuition to push you into your greatness. Stay in the AL Flow State, and the payoffs will come so much more quickly and with a fraction of the pain. Listen for the "whisper" and honor its guidance.

CHAPTER THIRTEEN

FEEDBACK LOOPS

The more we are true to ourselves, the more we can con-
nect with and contribute to the world.

—Brendon Burchard
Tweet 4:49 PM–25 Mar 2016

Feedback loops are an ever-present part of our lives. Most of us don't realize the extent of the role they play in our sense of direction and fulfillment. The more externally entrained we are, the more feedback loops have power over us. Have you ever had an idea you thought was genius and felt great about, but then once you shared it with a few others, your genius was either strengthened or broken down depending on their reactions? Feedback loops do play an obvious and important role keeping us on track and in check. If you have a propensity for outlandish ideas, your feedback loops can help you to stay grounded and put your energy in places that will lead to positive outcomes. On the other hand, they can also shut down your genius and keep you from developing amazing ideas.

Feedback loops are also the root of our addictions and compulsive behaviors. For example, when we behave in a way that is self-sacrificial and demands gratitude from others, we feel the high of a positive emotional response as dopamine is released into our bodies. This trains us to seek out more opportunities to feel this way. Once our body burns through the dopamine, we find ourselves dipping into the emotional valley that has always followed these types of highs. This can show up in essentially any area of our lives. It can be praise from a boss for selling out a coworker, inappropriately seeking out attention from a person who finds us attractive, obsessively winning at a game or sports— the list goes on indefinitely. You can find similar examples of situations that, in contrast, can be interacted with in a healthy way and kept in a balance. They may even help us find meaning in our lives. Even if we keep our balance, the feedback does still affect our choices of whether or not to engage in certain activities again, as well as the level of enjoyment we feel from them.

I have coached many entrepreneurs who have worked their butts off chasing their dream and then reached a crashing point. They have given their business everything they had and the results have not even come close to their expectations. This feedback has shifted their perspective around what was once their dream. They come to me feeling like they hate their work and wondering why they ever pursued it in the first place. The amount they have been giving is way out of balance with what they have been getting back. Their feedback loop is bringing them disappointment and frustration. In their minds, they are directly tying their feedback into their enjoyment. I always ask these clients the same question, "If your business started gaining traction and you had so many clients seeking out your services that you had to choose which ones to work with, how would you feel about your work?" They instantly light up and start sharing how much they love their work when it is successful. They move outside of the existing negative feedback loop and reengage with their passion.

When our feedback loops are primarily external, it is difficult for us to feel what we are really passionate about. Once we move into a more sovereign state, it shifts more of our feedback loops from external to internal. We still have to be practical in where we put our energy, but our truth and passions are not dictated as much by other people's responses. We are able to get in touch with who we are and what we enjoy in a much clearer and deeper way.

When we first start living in the AL Flow State, we find that the more often we do it, the longer we are able to maintain it. Then, at a certain point, we surpass the balancing point where we are in the AL Flow more often than we are not. At this point, instead of tracking how often we are able to maintain our alignment, we start becoming more aware of when we have popped out. As we progress, we notice the times we are out of alignment becoming shorter and shorter until it is a less common occurrence.

Sometimes clients misuse their skill of being able to transition in and out of alignment. They have the ability to pop out and live externally in the world when it feels good (positive feedback loop) and return to the AL Flow State the moment being external feels bad (negative feedback loop). It is common for clients to engage with their emotional addictions in this way. They selectively stay external for the high, and then realign to avoid the lows.

My client Cindy was a big people pleaser. One of her favorite feedback loops was to feel gratitude and acceptance from the people she would please. Of course being a people pleaser comes with a substantial downside. You find yourself giving and giving as you seek out approval from others. It is easy to let your own needs (and sometimes integrity) go because your need for gratitude and acceptance is overpowering your other needs. This was a pattern Cindy knew well and she hated the crash she would receive after burning through the feelings and neurophysiological release connected with being accepted and appreciated. She would slide into self-loathing as she recognized how poorly she treated herself and her coworkers to please her boss.

As she started her work with Aligned Living, she discovered what at first felt like the perfect workaround. Cindy would stay external as she pleased her boss and felt the recognition and gratitude. She would hop on the roller coaster for the fun part of the ride, the part she was addicted to. Then, she would feel her coworkers start to get annoyed with her and realize how she had sold out for the positive feedback loop. The moment the crash started to happen, she would jump off the roller coaster and move into the AL Flow State. From this place, she would rebalance herself and not have to take the roller coaster through to the negative swing. At first, Cindy had no idea she was even doing this.

Initially this might seem like a genius solution. You can engage in your addictive behavior and only experience the highs without having to deal with the lows. It's like only having to go to work on payday, and it sounds pretty enticing at first. But that's only until we take a deeper look at the cost of interacting in this way. Remember, the whole point of stepping into sovereignty was to be in charge of our own lives. When we engage with external feedback loops, they control us through our emotions. We start making choices and behaving in ways that don't serve our highest purpose or alignment. We let other people choose for us based on their external feedback loops. The boss who needs to be pleased controls Cindy by putting her into a people pleaser role. Each of our feedback loops driven by emotional addictions and compulsions fit together with our surroundings like the pieces of a puzzle.

Do you remember my client Samantha Skelly, owner of Hungry for Happiness, from the first chapter of this book? One of the things she told me is very applicable here: "Now I am better with boundaries in all areas of my life because I am clear about what I want. Interestingly, I don't have to set them very often. The new way I am being is teaching other people how to treat me. And they are responding." Often our biggest fears around disengaging from feedback loops are about setting boundaries and replacing the "high" we feel from the experience. Our EMFs naturally create new boundaries for us, and being in the AL Flow State gives us a "high."

The high we experience from being fully aligned is different from the high of an addictive behavior. The aligned high is sustainable and does not move us into an emotional state. We feel great and in control, and there is no compulsion to do something out of alignment. What we create from this place serves us well and sets us up for more positive experiences that seem to steadily get better. When we are in flow, life almost always feels good, regardless of what is going on outside of us. We have disconnected from being controlled by the feedback loops. The addictive or compulsive high may top out with a seemingly higher peak, but it is extremely short lived. I would also argue that the peak only feels higher because it is surrounded by lows. If we pop out of alignment for the high and back in to avoid the low, we start having experiences that are all over the place. Our foundation does not form in a solid enough way to create from because we gave up our sovereignty to engage with the feedback loops. We sold out.

CHAPTER FOURTEEN

CHOOSING YOUR BALLOONS

You are responsible for the energy that you create for yourself, and you're responsible for the energy that you bring to others.

—Oprah Winfrey
The Oprah Winfrey Show

You may have used affirmations in the past and wondered why some of them seem to create change while others bring frustration and disempowerment. This experience is not unique to you. Let me explain my understanding of what is happening. In order for something to occur in our lives, we have to be willing to let it happen. Most of us are in constant internal tug-of-wars with ourselves as our aspirations and fears struggle against each other.

Let's say you have decided you want to be a more influential leader that people look to for guidance. You may develop the affirmation, "People recognize my influence, look to me as a leader, and continuously seek me out as an authority." Now let's also say that you get nervous and uncomfortable when people you respect turn to you as an authority. Something in your self-worth gets triggered, and you defer the authority or self-sabotage the goal you are working to achieve. No matter how many times you look in the mirror and say, "People recognize my influence, look to me as a leader, and continuously seek me out as an authority," you won't become that authority.

First, you need to stop operating from the consciousness level and perspective that is undermining your goal. There is no magic bypass that will allow you to achieve what you want without shifting the part of you that is blocking it from happening. The good news is that when we stay in the AL Flow State, we don't concede to our old triggers, fears, and doubts.

I developed an exercise that will help you entrain with what you intend to create while simultaneously breaking your entrainments with what is holding you back. I call this exercise, "Choosing Your Balloons," and have found it to be far more successful than traditional affirmations. We choose what we entrain with just by thinking about it. When we think about something, we put our energy into it, we connect with it. We use our imagination to make it real in our energy field. We move into resonance with whatever it is we are thinking about, good or bad. We become entrained with the idea of whatever perspective we are bringing to the table, "My boss is a jerk," or "My coworkers are out to get me." We behave as if our thoughts are true, and our EMFs carry this information as well. As our behavior and EMFs interact with our surroundings, they become self-fulfilling. We often succumbed to our own power of suggestion, as does whatever surrounds us. This is why Choosing Your Balloons works.

In order to move forward with this exercise, you need to be able to hold the possibility that what I am about to say may be true and be willing to act as if it is true throughout the duration of this experiment. So much of what we consider "just the way things are" is created by our individual belief systems. If this were not true, how do you explain how differently each of us experience life? Why do some of us have challenge after challenge while others seem to receive nothing but support and positive outcomes? While this may be an exaggeration, "good luck" and "bad luck" are definitely not distributed equally.

What we believe to be a concrete reality about how the world treats us and what we get, is actually quite different from that. The reason it feels concrete is because we do such an amazing job of creating the same types of situations, relationships, and circumstances over and over again. Our "reality" is simply based on our individual experiences, what we have been taught, and how we have responded to life. It is as if we are positioned between two perfectly aligned mirrors that reflect back and forth between each other for infinity. One mirror is our individual "reality," and the other mirror is our consciousness. We aren't dummies. We see the reflections very clearly in this feedback loop. They continuously repeat and have done so throughout our lives. How could our reality not be the truth? Well, think about a breakthrough moment you had in your life, an epiphany that completely shifted your perspective about "the way things are." Your consciousness shifted and therefore your reality followed. You started experiencing "reality" differently. You changed the part of the equation you have control over, your consciousness.

When we move into our sovereign state, breaking our external entrainments and then open internally into the AL Flow State, we create an amazing opportunity to change the rules of our reality. Through this shift in consciousness, we gain the ability to change what is being reflected between the mirrors. Our conscious is no longer locked into whatever we were entrained with externally. We have broken the feedback loop. Now it is all happening internally. We are in control. Our EMF can become much clearer. We experience a massive expansion of what we feel we can create. Our intentions are no longer diluted by the influence of external EMFs.

At this point, most of us make some significant yet doable changes with a few mind-blowing shifts thrown in. This happens simply because we have now entrained with ourselves and the EMF of the earth (or the divine). The shifts that can happen are still limited by what we believe is possible and what we are willing to allow without self-sabotage. These beliefs and self-sabotages are really habits at this point. We continue to recreate the same patterns because we are not yet willing to allow for the shift in consciousness. We are too stuck in ordinary reality. We feel safe in it, despite the fact that we find so much of what we are experiencing to be extremely frustrating. So, like the soldier that just got back from basic training and still continues to make their bed perfectly and wake up ridiculously early regardless of how much they hate it, we continue with our conditioning. We continue operating in the old limitations that we were once entrained with. It takes a conscious effort to embrace the new freedom and control that is now available.

As clients start to realize they actually have access to the control panel that drives their reality, a whole new level of breakthrough becomes available. We have always known that the world responds to us the way we respond to the world, and we generally embrace the power of positive thinking. The big game changer, however, is that this shift in thinking is not only about how we perceive the world and how it responds to our actions; it is also about the influence of our EMF. The moment we take charge of our EMF, we take charge of our world.

Can you entertain the idea that what I just shared is true? Can you do it at least long enough to complete this experiment? I hope so, because I know what happens next. This exercise is based on the idea that whatever we choose to put our thoughts and energy into in our lives will grow. This becomes exponentially true the more we live in the AL Flow State. We will work with our intuitive self, the part of us that has a deeper sense of knowing, by asking it to show us what we have been entraining with. As we begin to understand what we are pouring our energy into, we will reflect on what it is creating in our lives. We will visualize that the energy we are putting out is filling different balloons. Each balloon represents something we are experiencing in our lives. Then we will check in to see if what we are creating feels in or out of resonance to our aligned state. If it feels in alignment, we will continue to feed it energy and keep that balloon full. If it feels out of alignment, we will let that balloon deflate and then either relabel the balloon and refill it or just discard it completely. The goal is to only fill the balloons that you want to either maintain or create more of in your life. If you don't want to create something anymore, then stop feeding it, stop filling the balloon!

This is also a great tool for monitoring your thoughts and seeing where your energy is going throughout the day. It is a perfect addition to your check-in routines throughout your day. A common question between practicers of Aligned Living is, "What balloons are you filling?"

When Maureen showed up to meditation, she was feeling pretty frustrated. It seemed like there was always some new drama at the office. Somebody always putting their own needs over the service they were supposed to be providing. This was a real pet peeve of Maureen's and quickly triggered her into judgment. She had also just happened to walk into the class in which I was introducing the "Choosing Your Balloons" exercise. She let go of her day as she settled into our visualization and the AL Flow State. She shared afterwards how surprised she was when she asked her intuitive self to show her what she had been entraining with. She realized there were dozens of potentially irritating things throughout her day that she could have been triggered into entraining with, but she hadn't. She didn't even have a balloon to represent them. These minor irritations just came and went throughout her day. The big balloon of self-involved behavior stayed with her all day and showed up in multiple places. She felt as if she was being "taunted by the universe." Throughout the exercise, she let her energy out of the "self-involved behavior" balloon and shifted herself to entrain with the more positive aspects of her job. She filled the balloons of "client appreciation" and "freedom in work schedule."

Maureen reported very little self-involved behavior showing up throughout the next week. When it did show up, it didn't feel personal, and she was able to let go of it with relative ease. She felt greater job satisfaction as she focused on her clients' appreciation and the freedom her schedule provided. Now of course when something is on our radar, we are far more likely to notice it, and when we are not too concerned about something, we are more likely to miss it completely. Our awareness is an easy way to explain why things shifted for Maureen after this exercise. There is another level to it however, that cannot simply be attributed to awareness. Her coworkers stopped bringing their self-involved tales of injustice to her. The moment she was no longer an energetic match, they moved on. She said it felt like her EMF was actually repelling them away from her desk. Maureen laughed to herself as she watched the same coworkers that drove her crazy last week walk right past her, bringing their stories down the hall to her friend Tony. They were drawn to him like a tractor beam, and she could see the irritation on his face.

Choosing Your Balloons Exercise

1) Complete the full Aligned Living visualization.
2) Settle into a meditative state as you get in touch with where your EMF runs through your brain and spinal column.
3) Ask your intuitive self to show you where you have been putting your energy.
4) Identify each place you have been putting your energy as a separate balloon and label it.
5) Bring the balloon into your alignment and see how it shows up for you. Does it feel in complete alignment? Then visualize yourself continuing to fill it and stay entrained with it. Does it feel mostly in alignment? Ask your intuitive self what needs to change about the balloon. Imagine yourself making those changes, and relabel the balloon. Does it feel completely out of alignment? See yourself letting your energy out of the balloon. Then choose to either discard the balloon or relabel and refill it.
6) Spend some time in your meditative state visualizing your thoughts and EMF shifting into this new, greater alignment.

Keep these balloons in your conscious awareness and check in with them throughout your day. You will start to catch yourself when you begin refilling old balloons you have committed to discarding. When you find yourself in your old pattern, just stop, choose differently, and celebrate the change you are making. Berating yourself for falling into old patterns fills a balloon with energy you don't want in your life.

CHAPTER FIFTEEN

COMMITTING TO ROUTINES

Commit to showing up with full vitality and excellence each day and a funny thing happens: Your life becomes vibrant and extraordinary.

—Brendon Burchard
Inspirational Brendon Burchard Quotes on Success

A s we saw with Sherry in chapter eleven and with so many other clients, change can happen instantly but we won't be able to sustain it without commitment. There is only a very short period with this work where mind over matter is needed to move into the AL Flow State. Once we enter that state of consciousness, our instincts and desires quickly change as well. This is why so many clients experience success in breaking habits they have been struggling to change for years. Of course the moment we let ourselves slide or get triggered out of our alignment, we have to rely on our awareness and willpower to make the conscious choice to realign. That is, until realigning becomes an ingrained habit.

I developed a technique my clients have found to be extremely helpful when needing to call on their willpower. When a habit we are trying to break presents itself to us, it shows up like a salesperson. It presents us with everything we find alluring about it. We entrain with the payoffs and may trick ourselves into thinking it is the right choice in the moment. Then buyer's remorse often kicks in. When you go to the BMW dealer the salesperson does not talk about how their cars have low dependability ratings or how pricey they are to service. They lead with their strong suits. "Have you ever driven a BMW? Let's get you behind the wheel so you can experience it." For many, the less than stellar dependability rating and high cost of repairs is easy to overlook for the reward of how they feel to drive. The salesperson's job is to give you an emotional experience with the car. This is the place most people make decisions from. They feel impulsive inside the rush of the experience and are more likely to make the purchase. So whether you are buying a BMW, engaging in an old habit, abandoning your diet, indulging in gossip, or engaging in anger, emotion is most likely the driver that makes it feel like the right choice in the moment.

We can train ourselves to recognize this moment and take one simple step. When we recognizing we are entraining with the "payoff," we can move our focus to the bigger picture. We can fast-forward to that moment when the buyer's remorse normally kicks in. As we bring that moment into our awareness, we gain access to the bigger picture. We get to tap into the whole experience rather than just the payoff. This technique has a "sobering" effect, and the emotional charge often dissipates, allowing us to make a grounded choice rather than diving in on an emotional high. When we take this step, something profound happens. Our trust in our self grows. This increases our self-esteem and therefore our confidence. This becomes one more piece in the puzzle to showing up fully, trusting your insight, and embodying your influence. You will be taking one step deeper into your personal power.

This chapter is dedicated to assisting you in creating routines you can commit to. At the end of this chapter, you will find a template to help you create your routines. (It is also available in the appendix at the back of this book.) Having a written plan is a huge support to reference in those moments when your foundation feels shaky and to proactively keep that from happening in the first place.

All of the routines are important, but the morning routine definitely carries the biggest impact. When you first wake up you can either take charge and choose what you entrain with, or just let it go to default and see what shows up. How many times have you woken up and without a thought grabbed your phone and checked texts, emails, or the news? You're in a susceptible state to be drawn into whatever shows up, and you know it can set the tone for your day. For this reason, it is so important to take charge of the first few minutes of your morning.

I recommend you start each day with the full Aligned Living visualization. At first use the recording, but as you develop your own process over time, you may no longer need it. The recording can bring an extra level of support. On days I am feeling a bit challenged in bringing myself into the AL Flow State, I still call on the recording. Your morning routine can include several additional steps to support yourself in staying in the AL Flow State throughout the day. In the past, many clients added affirmations. This technique for entraining with what we intend to create has become common practice for many business professionals with a widely varying degree of success. As I shared in the last chapter, I recommend replacing affirmations with Choosing Your Balloons exercise. I use this technique regularly with my clients and for myself, and I find it far more effective than affirmations.

Adding some sort of physical movement such as yoga, stretching, or other exercise is also very effective. Clients who have never been in touch with their physical bodies are often surprised at how this shifts as they begin living in the AL Flow State. Our bodies are meant to support us, and the more we are aligned the more this will happen. These exercises can be short and simple. In fact, I recommend that all the routines you set up should feel easy and not daunting. If we experience internal resistance to doing them, we most likely will not stick with it. If you are having to use a lot of willpower to stick with your routines, you need to change them to feel more supportive. Let them shift into something you want to do and you will be more likely to do them.

Throughout the day, regular check-ins are necessary to maintain your alignment. You can use specific times, but I find it more effective to utilize natural transition points. You can use your existing routines such as meetings, connecting with clients, or work breaks to structure your check-in times. A check-in should include going internal for a moment and seeing if you have any leaks or areas you are externally entrained. If so, shut them down and reopen internally. Next, see how you are feeling. Is your EMF flowing, can you tap in with the euphoric sensations, is the energy running smoothly through your brain, spinal column, and spine? If not, take the necessary steps to move back into the AL Flow State. I always take these steps prior to an important meeting, phone call, or any situation I am knowingly walking into where I want to be at my best.

Establishing a bedtime routine is another important factor. How many times have you felt the state of mind you went to bed in affect your sleep and dreams? When we are feeling a bit sideways, even when we are sleeping, our hearts and brains are out of coherence, and in turn our EMF is not supporting us. You will find you are far more likely to sleep well and wake up in the morning with greater clarity, insight, and often solutions to challenges in all areas of your life if you align before bed. When you take a few minutes to go through your visualizations and fall asleep in a meditative state, you support yourself to be in the AL Flow State throughout the night. It is a wonderful feeling to wake up with your entire EMF already in alignment and your heart and brain in full coherence.

The final suggestion I will offer in committing to your routines is finding an accountability partner. I will lead by saying that this step is not for everybody. Be honest with yourself here as you check in to see if an accountability partner will serve you well. What is your track record with sticking to commitments? Are you somebody who sets their mind to something and then follows through? Are you somebody who has great intentions but tends to lose track of them? Does the thought of an accountability partner feel supportive? If not, is it because you work best on your own, or is it because it is uncomfortable to be called out? If you find yourself trying to avoid the accountability, you are probably somebody who would really benefit from working with a partner. I have always been a person who prefers to go it alone, but working with Aligned Living has been an exception for me. The more I connect with others who are also aligned, the easier it is for me to stay in the AL Flow State, and the more powerful it feels.

However you choose to proceed is up to you. The information here is about giving you the most supportive and effective path forward. Clients who don't create new routines and habits for themselves generally see less significant results and are more likely to slide back into old ways of being. I also conduct weekly Aligned Living coaching groups that include the AL meditation visualization. There is no doubt that the people who join us each week either in person or online are experiencing exponential growth. Their commitment is the key.

Daily Routines Template

Morning Routine:
-Aligned Living meditation: What works best for you? A recording on your phone? Taking yourself through the meditation?

_____

-Filling Your Balloons: Does it work best for you to write them out first? Do they just show up for you in meditation? What are the balloons that you fill every day?

_____

_____

_____

_____

-Are you adding a physical element such as yoga, stretching, or exercise?

_____

_____

Throughout the Day:
-What works best to remind you to check in on your alignment? Do you have natural breaks in your day? Do you check in before engaging with clients or coworkers? What is your plan?

_____

_____

Bedtime:
-What is your commitment to making sure you are going to sleep in an aligned state? Will you use a recording or take yourself through the meditation? Does it work best for you to do the meditation in bed or before going to bed?

_____

_____

_____

CHAPTER SIXTEEN

CHOOSING YOUR ALIGNMENT EXERCISES

In theory, there is no difference between theory and practice. But in practice, there is.

—Jan L. A. van de Snepscheut
Computer scientist

The most common challenge I see clients face is choosing to stay aligned internally rather than giving in to the temptation to entrain with the external. Of course we all want to be able to snap our fingers and simply live in the AL Flow State. While a small percentage of people manage to do that, for the large majority it takes persistence. Not pushing, just persistence. We need to monitor where we are entrained. If we find ourselves external, acknowledge it and reset. Getting angry, frustrated, or moving into self-judgment is the opposite of what we are working towards. The most effective response to sliding into external entrainment is to take a minute and ask yourself a few questions: How do I feel in my body right now? What am I currently creating? How do I want to feel, and what do I want to create? Realign and fill those balloons. What follows are several exercises to assist you in changing your old habit.

The News: I generally get my news from articles on the internet rather than watching it on TV or online videos. Television news is filled with sensationalism and drama. It contains constant invitations to entrain with fear and negativity. This is also what makes it a perfect training ground to practice staying aligned.

-Bring yourself into the AL Flow State giving particular intention to being internally entrained.

-Turn on the news and listen closely to the stories, being sure to pick up the details of what they are sharing.

-Monitor your internal state. There is a natural tendency to either entrain with the story or else to push it away, telling yourself why this couldn't happen to you in an attempt to disassociate yourself from the threat. This common defense mechanism is still keeping you from entraining with yourself. You are leaving your alignment so you can feel safe. When you disconnect you lose compassion and empathy for the people involved. Our goal is to stay aligned, take in the information, and simply be aware of it. You may think this would make you feel self-centered and uncaring, but that is not the case. Most people are amazed at how clear and capable they feel once they master this alignment. They find themselves being able to be more supportive. Maybe even take caring actions because they are not overwhelmed by the situation or disassociated from it.

Coffee Shops and Restaurants: I'm sure you have found yourself eavesdropping on conversations around you when you are visiting restaurants and coffee shops. Sometimes it is hard not to, and sometimes we do it on purpose. This is a perfect setting for practicing alignment and getting in touch with what is happening internally for you—what you are just allowing to happen, and the internal experience you are intentionally choosing. Are you going into judgment? "Well of course he doesn't treat her with respect. She obviously slept with him the night she met him." Or worrying, "I hope her son isn't lying to her." Our goal is to keep our alignment and to stay entrained with ourselves while we observe what is happening around us. Let other people's experiences, triumphs, and lessons be theirs, while you experience your own.

Driving in Traffic: This one has been my biggest challenge. Did I mention I live in Southern California? This exercise is only effective if you are somebody who gets triggered by inconsiderate or aloof drivers and lives somewhere that traffic gets congested. If this doesn't describe you, feel free to skip to the next exercise.

-Bring yourself into the AL Flow State giving particular intention to being internally entrained. Be careful not to go too deep—safe driving is your priority.

-As you drive through traffic, practice an awareness of other drivers, but keep your focus on being positive and aligned.

-If you find yourself going into "stories" about other drivers, stop, visualize yourself (with your eyes open) disconnecting and moving back into sovereignty. Your story about them is not doing anything positive.

-As you drive through traffic, monitor where your mind is naturally wanting to take you and practice taking charge of your thoughts. If you find yourself externally entrained, reset and play the game again.

Work Meetings: For many of us, work meetings can take us to a lot of places. How have your work meetings been lately? This is a perfect place to practice your alignment. It is also a place where your new sense of authority can be practiced as well.

Shower Water Temperatures or Getting in the Pool: Whenever I would get into water for a swim, my body used to instantly hyperventilate. My system was extremely reactive compared to most, but I know we all go through a certain level of discomfort when entering the water or getting into a cold shower. The idea for this exercise came about when our water heater broke. I needed to shower, but didn't have any hot water. I realized this was a perfect time to test the entrainment theory and bring in a physical, rather than just psychological, element to it. I was amazed as I was able to align and hold that internal entrainment while getting into the cold shower. I took a few deep breaths, and I was fine. Yes, I was very aware that the water was cold, but when I entrained on my internal warmth rather than the external cold, I was fine—no hyperventilating, no swearing, just breathing. Now I use this technique whenever I get in the cold Pacific Ocean. I never could have imagined that not hyperventilating was simply a choice.

CHAPTER SEVENTEEN

COMMON CHALLENGES

Happiness is not the absence of problems; it's the ability to deal with them.

—Steve Maraboli
Life, the Truth, and Being Free

When business professionals are asked about their primary work concerns, there are themes that universally show up. These include: feeling pressured by work situations or by their direct report to do more with less and to pass this pressure on to others; the absence of a clear vision; and constant reconfiguring of personnel, departments, and direction. These challenges all boil down to a feeling of being squeezed. This squeeze throws people into conditioned fear-based behavior, where their thinking and actions become more unconscious. They come from everywhere but their center.

Under this stress we tend to focus on the idea that things are not yet how they are supposed to be, that something is wrong, and there is an action we need to take to correct this. For instance, I haven't closed enough deals, my report doesn't feel thorough enough, that client hasn't called back yet so I should give them another call, etc. While these may be real concerns and something may need to change, we aren't going to correct the problem by simply pushing forward. Particularly if we plan on doing so from an unaligned place where most of our impetus is coming from the need to alleviate the discomfort of "something is wrong." This type of suffering is really a state of mind that we are holding. We become committed to the idea that things are not how they are supposed to be. The difference between the thought that things are not the way they are supposed to be and the idea that "everything is okay" is a mental construct. When we remain attached to the perspective that something is wrong, we experience suffering.

Sure, you can say, "I missed my sales numbers, how is that okay? I should be upset!" or "I just lost my biggest client. Don't tell me everything is okay. I have every right to be freaking out!" Yes, you do have every right to be freaking out. Ask yourself this, however: what does it do for you to exercise that right? The moment you decide something is not okay you become entrained in that microcosm and lose touch with your greater reality. Instantly, it's not just something that is not okay, everything is not okay. Your thinking shifts, you lose your alignment and perspective, and you start creating from that unaligned place.

It is easy to forget that we do get to choose our states of consciousness. We "have a right" to turn down invitations to feel ways we don't want to feel. We have the right to stay entrained with a greater sense of self, rather than shrinking into the smallness of a moment. We should start to see every invitation to entrain with a small moment as boiled potatoes. (No sour cream, no bacon, no chives, just boiled potatoes.) Not too many of us have a strong reaction to boiled potatoes. The choice to eat boiled potatoes is not emotionally driven. We are not likely to say, "I'm stuffed but I can't resist another bite of boiled potatoes!" If it were ice cream, pizza, or fudge, on the other hand, you might say, "Ooh fudge, I'm full but I can always make room for fudge!" Negative emotions are never fudge, so don't make room for them. So, when you don't close that deal, what next step is going to serve you best? We will answer that question in the next chapter. First, let's examine a few ways people tend to respond to challenging situations. As we learn to live in the AL Flow State, it becomes very clear to us whether we are in our channel of alignment or out of it. There are three different places we operate from once we have this awareness. Of course, being centered in our channel of flow is our goal, but even the best of us find ourselves slipping out of alignment from time to time. The other two places we end up in, I refer to as "Pushing against the Cage" and "Being Pushed by the Cage."

When we are "Pushing against the Cage" we have lost trust and left our center. We find ourselves operating externally and trying to change what we are experiencing, not from alignment, but in a desperate way. We have defaulted into the "something's wrong and I better freak out about it" place. We have traded in our alignment to step into the role of "The Meddler." The entire next chapter is dedicated to understanding that role, so I won't go into too much detail about it here. Let me just say that when we start pushing against the cage, we tend to become more emotional and diminish our clarity, authority, and influence. We become entrained with our obstacles, and it can feel impossible to set boundaries as the demands of the world appear to close in around us. We let go of the bigger picture and shrink our perception of the world until we are completely engulfed in the challenge.

While "Pushing against The Cage" is about misaligned action, "Being Pushed by the Cage" is about misaligned inaction. It is the feeling of knowing you need to be doing something but are avoiding or resisting the action that you know will maintain your alignment. This is usually triggered by a fear of stepping into the spotlight or shouldering greater responsibilities. From our centered place, we know we are ready, but we have let fear get the best of us and have gone into resistance and self-sabotage. We are trying to reject the natural progression that comes with the growth we have made. The more we develop our awareness, the easier it is to recognize when we are out of our alignment and dismantling what we have worked so hard to create.

Sometimes we take this to extremes. I heard this story while attending a Toastmasters International group, and I think it illustrates this concept perfectly. A woman was speaking who had joined the group over a year before. She had an intense fear of public speaking and was pushing herself to break through it. She nervously described her journey with Toastmasters, relating how the first time she was scheduled to speak, she had a car accident while driving to the event. She simply drove off the side of the road, but she had no idea how it had happened. She remembered being in a panicky state thinking about standing in front of a small group of people delivering her speech, and the next thing she knew she was down a bank with her car smashed against a tree. Luckily, she was relatively unharmed. She had joined Toastmasters in a fairly aligned state, but when it came time to step up, she panicked and tried to escape. Her speech was rescheduled for another evening and she ended up coming down with a stomach bug that afternoon and having to reschedule again. She was finally able to deliver her speech on her third attempt. (It may have helped that she had a friend drive her there.) She didn't win any ribbons, but she forced herself to get up and do it. The whole time she was "Being Pushed by the Cage." I commend her for overcoming her fear as she did. I also know how much more powerful we can feel when we confront our fears from the AL Flow State.

CHAPTER EIGHTEEN

THE MEDDLER

Planetologist call it the conundrum of unforeseen ecological consequence. I call it the whack-a-mole rule of human meddling.... WHACK! We change something here. Oops, that makes another problem pop up there where we didn't expect it. WHACK! So, we whack that mole. Oops! We're so smart that we're a menace.

—Robert Buettner
Overkill

There is a natural tendency to move into the role I call, "The Meddler." Meddlers are seldom patient. Their actions are driven by an internal discomfort. They often feel a sense of urgency to keep changing things with the intention that somehow this push will solve the perceived problem and alleviate the discomfort. Generally, this becomes an out of the frying pan and into the fire type of experience. Meddlers tend to skip the planning phase. They like to move right into action. Essentially, their meddling is driven by emotions not logic.

From my experiences with my clients as well as in my own life, I think it is fair to say that about 10 to 20 percent of our actions create about 90 percent of our results. This means that about 80 to 90 percent of the actions we take aren't really creating anything positive. We are often just taking them in an attempt to alleviate an inner discomfort. A feeling that things are not the way they should be. This 80 to 90 percent is the domain of the Meddler, who is constantly taking action to alleviate a discomfort only to replace it with a new suffering. The Meddler is not only ineffective, it often does damage by reducing the effectiveness of what we have already created. It undoes what we have already aligned. Most of us hold a lot of illusion about how effective the Meddler is. When we are operating in the AL Flow State that illusion breaks. Once we see how much we undermine our own self-interest, the Meddler moves from our go-to way of being, to our biggest nemesis and a role that we avoid at all costs.

Back to the question, then, from the last chapter: "When you don't close that deal, what next step is going to serve you best?" The next step is stopping what you are doing and bringing yourself back into alignment. Move back into the AL Flow State. You can fulfill your urgency and need for action by letting that action be our alignment visualization. For many people, this takes practice. You may need to have some experiences with not aligning first. You may tell yourself, "I don't have time for that alignment stuff right now. I need to fix this." Then you can run forward and create a bigger mess. Maybe you can scare away your next big potential client when they witness you in a place of emotionally-driven desperation. You might need to go show your boss, coworkers, direct reports, or employees what you look like when you are freaking out. You may have to invite them to question your capabilities and natural authority. If you are feeling the need to self-sabotage in that way, go ahead. It is an important step in the process. Then come back and ask yourself, "How did that work out for me?" Sometimes we need to really screw things up in order to find the value of growing to the next level.

Once you move past the first level of self-sabotage and experience the results of maintaining the AL Flow State, there can be a tendency to forget how you earned it. I see so many clients lose track of the fundamentals of staying aligned. They get caught up in the high of riding the wave of success. Within weeks of starting flow work my client Brian reported back to me how amazed he was at his sudden jump in success. New clients were showing up like he had never experienced before. On top of that, they were almost exclusively high-end clients, the kind of client you can make a career on—and not just one, but three separate opportunities showed up all at once. His boss was dumbfounded as well and asked Brian, "How did you land these clients? They are way above even my pay grade." Brian was seeing and experiencing what was possible. Living in alignment was paying off quickly. He decided to celebrate by taking off for the weekend with some friends. He had a blast partying and connecting with people he really enjoyed. He found himself deep in their world. Throughout the weekend, he slowly became entrained with their struggles and concerns. It felt good to be helpful, and it was easy for him to do. He came back from the weekend feeling great about his connection with others but disconnected from himself. His work week started off slow, the flow of new clients had suddenly stopped, and he wasn't hearing back from his new high-end clients.

Brian came into his next session with me a bit rattled, wondering how things could change so quickly. As we sat down it was easy to tell that Brian was out of his alignment and flow. It quickly became apparent to Brian what he had done. The fear that he had screwed up the success he had just created became palpable. We spent a few minutes moving back into the AL Flow State. It was like thinking a light was broken only to realize it wasn't plugged in. Brian lit up and instantly had a new perspective and plan forward. By the next day, his big clients were back in touch with him and the flow of new clients and opportunities had restarted.

It is important to note here that the problem was not that Brian had taken off to celebrate with his friends. The problem was that he had let go of his greater sense of self. His friends were not living in the AL Flow State, so of course they were entrained with the drama in their lives. They were not seeing a greater sense of themselves, but rather getting stuck in "what's wrong." Instead of staying aligned, Brian left his center and joined his friends. His EMF matched up with their struggles. This resonance felt beautiful in the moment, but came with consequences. Brian has now committed to keeping his alignment and assisting his friends by inviting them to join him in a centered place rather than going sideways himself to connect.

Brian had experienced an invitation to engage in what felt like a positive way. More frequently we see invitations to engage in negative ways. My client Bill had a coworker, Jan, who seemed to have it out for him. Every time Bill presented an idea in a meeting or had a project he was pitching, Jan would have a problem with it. Despite being at the same level, she would talk condescendingly to Bill as if she were his boss. This started on Bill's first day at work and hadn't let up. Bill had a long history of having a nemesis everywhere he worked. This time it was Jan. The moment their EMFs overlapped, disharmony occurred. They were not in resonance with each other at all. Bill had responded in his old way. He decided Jan was always going to be a problem. He would unconsciously place all his attention on her EMF. He wouldn't entrain with it, but rather, he would battle with it. He would fight to hold his own and attempt to not let her upset him while at the same time focusing on everything he disliked about her. It was like driving by an accident and trying not to look. Jan responded to Bill in a very similar way. Together they created a disharmonic field which they each continuously fed into. It was the one "project" they were great at collaborating on.

As Bill learned about living in his alignment and the AL Flow State, he started to see his role in their "project." He realized that he was constantly feeding energy into it and "filling the balloon." It became clear to Bill that he was caught up in the idea that Jan had started it and had caused this same problem for quite a few of their coworkers. This, along with his certainty that she was to blame, was the evidence he was using to maintain his role in their antagonism toward each other. I asked Bill how he felt when he was around Jan or even thought of her. His expression instantly changed and his EMF radiated anger and injustice. He felt really uncomfortable to be around. I shared how it felt for me to be around him at that moment and how he usually felt really good to be around. The next question I asked him triggered an epiphany. "Bill, how does it feel to be in your body right now?" He sat there for a minute, tempted to reiterate how it was Jan's fault. As he stopped himself, I could see the truth come over him. He didn't feel crappy right now because of Jan. He felt crappy because he had chosen to engage in their "project" together, to entrain in their battle. We both thought it was humorous that they had refused to work together on any other projects, but this one had been both of their highest priorities.

Like most of us, Bill was operating from the perspective that other people make us feel different emotions depending on how they treat us, and that external relationships control our internal state of being. When we operate out of alignment and outside of the AL Flow State, this is completely true. The moment we bring ourselves internal and into flow, this truth changes. From this state of consciousness our internal harmony drives the external. We make the realization that how we feel is a result of our relationship with our self, not with anything external.

This truth is easier to exercise in some situations than in others. If we are dealing with a nasty coworker or neighbor, it is a lot easier to let them stay external and create their own problems. When you are engaging with somebody you have deep feelings for, it raises the stakes. This adds a whole other level of trust to your flow work and usually takes more time to develop. For most people, accepting that it is okay to have a situation with a loved one and not run the pain of it through their emotional body feels counterinstinctual. It feels like if they aren't suffering in it, they aren't showing they care or how "important" the situation is. If that is your experience, then please do honor it. I have, however, witnessed many clients who, over time, are able to maintain the AL Flow State even in the face of challenging situations with loved ones. They operate from the perspective that they can have a deeper understanding and be a much bigger support to themselves and their loved ones when they don't accept the invitation to go into suffering.

In this case, Bill disengaged from the "project" and eventually Jan lost interest in him. She moved onto her next nemesis. Bill had broken his pattern. He also got to witness her recreate the same situation with a different coworker. It was never about her relationship with him or even his with her. It was about what they were each looking for. Since they were both unknowingly looking for a battle, a nemesis, they locked in on each other and created just that. The moment Bill shifted his alignment, and therefore his EMF, he was no longer a match. Their "project" fell apart. By living in the AL Flow State, he became much more energetically clean. Before his EMF attracted resistance and battle. Now it attracts support and, at the same time, repels resistance through the "Tractor Beam" and the "Gift of Rejection."

CHAPTER NINETEEN

THE TRACTOR BEAM AND THE GIFT OF REJECTION

Find out who you are and do it on purpose.

—Dolly Parton

The Tractor Beam

We have all had the experience of feeling instantly attracted to a person, group, situation, or even a place. The moment you became aware of it, you were drawn in, as if you were being pulled by a tractor beam. This is the experience of resonance. When your EMF matches the frequency of something external, there is a palpable lock in, like a much subtler version of singing with somebody and hitting the same note. This phenomenon exists whether you are in or out of alignment with yourself. What you are in resonance with is always a perfect match for your EMF in that moment. The problem is, until you align and move into the AL Flow State, your EMF is going to be attuned with your old experiences and therefore attract and recreate them over and over again. The patterns each of us repeat in our lives are fairly predictable and frustrating. Think of one of your closest friends or family members. What are their top three patterns? Pretty easy to identify, right? So are yours, and mine, and everybody else's. I call it "taking another lap." I often jokingly ask clients, "Are you done with that pattern yet, or would you like to take another lap?"

These patterns can be difficult to break, and this is why. When we let our EMF carry the frequencies that naturally show up, they are a reflection of our past experiences and what we surround ourselves with. Since we attract in what is in resonance with us, what we surround ourselves with is simply a reflection of our past. This is why change can be so difficult. We are each the less destructive version (hopefully) of a person coming out of rehab and trying to be clean while going back into their old surroundings. There is a reason these people are instructed to change where they live and who they spend time with.

The good news is we don't have to move, cut people out of our lives, or take a different job to create this same change. (Although, don't be surprised if some of that naturally happens as you discover what does and does not align with the true you.) We can create this change by disengaging our emotional bodies from the external, aligning ourselves, moving into the AL Flow State, and being aware of which "balloons" we are filling. These simple steps instantly change our EMF and engage the Tractor Beam. Our old patterns don't feel as familiar anymore. In fact, as you probably already experienced, it is difficult to connect with the old drama, as if you can't find your access to it. Of course, you can just pop back out of alignment and recreate it, but why would you want to do that? Actually, there are a few reasons (none of them are good though). We will take a look at them shortly, but first let's look at the Gift of Rejection.

The Gift of Rejection

Those of us that are engaged in flow work love to celebrate the incredible connections and opportunities that it creates. This kind of clarity calls in those perfect matches and at the same time makes it really clear what is not in resonance. For many of us, particularly if we have a strong awareness of others, we can easily pick up on how we are being received. Most of us have a natural tendency to want to be liked. Through our awareness of who others want us to be, it is easy to unconsciously leave our alignment and adjust how we are presenting ourselves. We begin letting go of our true selves and start being more and more who the person we were connecting with wants us to be. As a payoff, they become more interested in us and, in a sense, choose us to connect with.

This seems to either be completely true for people or completely not true. Some people operate with the gift of rejection from the opposite end of the spectrum. They don't want to waste their time and energy with somebody or a situation that is out of resonance for them. They don't give people their energy, and as a result are often received as dismissive or arrogant. They forcefully do the rejecting themselves, then justify it with the idea that they have more important things to do and can't let other people hijack their time or attention. The people trying to connect with them show up as a threat. The common idea of, "I need to put up big boundaries and push this person away or they are going to take something from me," drives the harshness of the rejection.

Whenever we react out of fear, we are definitely operating out of alignment. The other person or people involved get a sense of this, and disharmony ensues. People who operate in this way usually don't stick around in the disharmony, so they don't realize the wake they are leaving behind them or the impact it is actually having on them. Being actively dismissive is disempowering to both parties. It shows we don't feel confident and powerful enough to hold our own so we need to be at least mildly abrasive to protect ourselves. When we stay aligned, there is no threat that somebody is going to steal our time or energy unless we allow them to. We don't need to be dismissive or condescending to protect ourselves. If this describes how you have protected yourself in the past, then the Gift of Rejection can maintain your boundaries without leaving the wake of disharmony behind you. That wake, and how it affects others, always comes back around to bite us.

If you are somebody who naturally adjusts yourself to make others comfortable or to be liked or "chosen," mastering the gift of rejection will allow you to connect with the right people and situations rather than ending up where others want you to be. Think about how often you have been at a party or other social situation and somebody started talking to you who you weren't interested in connecting with. It may have felt awkward, so you acted interested, maybe even asked questions trying to make it more comfortable. You ended up adjusting yourself and moving out of your alignment to make the other person comfortable. You didn't want to reject them, so instead you sacrificed yourself. This is common for those of us that have a natural tendency to leave our alignment and entrain with the EMF of others. We tap in with their awkwardness. It feels extremely uncomfortable to us, so we try to fix it. Congratulations, now you are their temporary best friend. You made them feel comfortable and signed yourself up for that job until you can find a way to excuse yourself.

Whenever I share this concept in workshops, I look around the room and see the realization in the faces of the folks that match what I just described. They realize they are not being trapped by others, but are adjusting themselves so the other person doesn't want them to leave. What would have happened if they had just stayed aligned? They could have had a short, maybe slightly awkward, and polite conversation, and both parties could have moved on to somebody they felt in resonance with. When we stop adjusting our own EMF and behavior to move into resonance with others, we experience a slight disharmony.

We don't get picked, both parties move on and we experience, the Gift of Rejection. We have a three-minute conversation rather than an hour one.

My favorite response to the Gift of Rejection occurred during a workshop I was leading. As I was sharing this concept, I looked around the room and saw a woman sitting with her jaw wide open. She had realized how much she naturally adjusted herself to make others more comfortable. I asked her if she was okay. She responded with, "I'm just realizing that if I practiced the Gift of Rejection in my past how different my life would be. I had a conversation with a guy at a party that should have ended after ten minutes, but instead turned into a ten-year marriage!"

The Gift of Rejection can be practiced in many aspects of our lives. A while back, my wife and I took our daughters to Hollywood Boulevard to walk around as tourists, take it all in, and visit the Walk of Fame. As you walk down the street, there are celebrity impersonators, buskers, people selling tours, and about everything else you could imagine. It was interesting to watch the different ways tourists would deal with these situations. Some didn't look at the performers (or allow themselves to be entertained), others snuck peeks, some hid behind the crowd for protection, some people engaged but then couldn't figure out how to get away, many opened their wallets to buy their release, and a few even became abusive. It was fascinating to me as I watched each tourist respond to the different characters making their living on Hollywood Boulevard in different ways.

In the midst of all the fear and curiosity, there was another small select group of people—the ones who felt confident and in charge of themselves. They were clear that the Don King impersonator could not make them take a picture with him, *Top Gun's* "Goose" could not convince them to change their sexual orientation, and no salesperson could make them board a bus to drive by the homes of celebrities. They were able to enjoy the show, stay aligned, engage in whatever way they wanted, choose whether or not to tip or purchase something, and then move on. There was no threat perceived. They knew they were in charge. Try this next time you are in a similar situation. It is a great place to exercise your own authority, and it will make the whole experience enjoyable, like a game. The most fascinating part is how different the "salespeople" treat you when they can feel you are not open to being pushed around. They tend to have fun with you, rather than attempting to influence you. In a sense, they acknowledge and honor your personal power and authority.

The Microscope Syndrome

As you step into flow work and the level of self-awareness it provides, let me share a quick warning about something I call the "Microscope Syndrome." I have always had a love for playing sports and played soccer throughout college. When I became a middle and high school teacher, it provided the opportunity for me to be the varsity boys' soccer coach. I placed a lot of emphasis on helping my players not just develop their physical skills, but also their knowledge and awareness of the mental aspects of the game. Inevitably, part way through the season, my top players would reach an internal crisis. It seemed like the cockier they were when they showed up to play for me, the harder it would hit them. I can recall a conversation I had with Mike, a self-proclaimed "phenom" player who stepped up to varsity as a freshman.

"I'm not sure what is going on coach," Mike told me. "I used to be so much better of a player. Now I feel like I am constantly screwing something up."

I replied, "That's interesting Mike, because from my perspective you are ten times the player you were at the beginning of the season. When we started, you were only focused on yourself and your stats. You felt like your only job was to score goals. As you started to see yourself as part of a team, your role expanded. You started to see how you could support your teammates. You realized you had a lot more to offer them. As you have been working at this, you are making the team more successful. Now that you can see what is possible, you are expecting a lot more from yourself. Your reflection on your play used to consist of, 'Did I score or not?' Now you see so many more ways you can lead and be powerful. You have moved from a broad reflection of your success to a much more magnified one. Your awareness has grown. It is as if you are looking at yourself under a microscope. You are scoring about the same number of goals as you were before, but feel like there is always something you could be doing better."

As your awareness grows, so will your sense of what is possible. Make sure you take the time to step back from the "microscope" and see how differently you are interacting in your world and what you have already created.

CHAPTER TWENTY

THE DANGERS OF MAGICAL THINKING

If you go back a few hundred years, what we take for granted today would seem like magic—being able to talk to people over long distances, to transmit images, flying, accessing vast amounts of data like an oracle. These are all things that would have been considered magic a few hundred years ago.

—Elon Musk
Forbes interview, March 23, 2013

As we dive deeper into flow work our reality starts to feel different than we have ever known it. As we observe ourselves creating unprecedented growth there is a danger, even for the most grounded and skeptical of us, to move into magical thinking. Magical thinking happens when we forget that we are creating these changes. Since so much of what we are doing is happening within what we have known as our imagination and in the unseen world of electromagnetic frequencies, it can feel like there is something magical happening. Whether it is magical or not depends on your perspective and definition of magic. If you are doing the Aligned Living work but not letting your understanding of the science of coherence fields and EMFs advance, then how do you explain what is happening? How do you fully own your role in it? Oddly enough, for many people it is easier for their mind to slip into the perspective of magical thinking than it is for them to expand their understanding of science.

I believe this is true for a couple reasons. First, the scientific community has traditionally presented itself with great authority and certainty as to having the right answers. They have also been slow to change their perspective, even when confronted with new information that contradicts previous theories. Scientists who have pioneered breakthroughs have generally been initially viewed as ridiculous, even dangerous, and scoffed at by their colleagues. Many scientists have lost their funding or positions in universities by heading down a path of inquiry that contradicts currently accepted scientific "facts."

The second primary factor that makes magical thinking so easy for people to slip into is the truth that most of us know there is more going on than our science textbooks can explain. When you or somebody you fully trust has had experiences outside of the realm of our current scientific models, at some level you reserve the space for magical thinking. A Gallup Poll was conducted in June of 2005 examining American's beliefs about the paranormal. They interviewed over 1,000 adults nationwide by asking them a series of yes or no questions about their paranormal beliefs. The results showed that about three in four Americans hold at least one paranormal belief. At this time, we don't have an accepted scientific explanation for the paranormal. For these three out of four Americans their only option is to accept that something is going on that science cannot or is unwilling to explain. The natural opening here is to move into the perspective that what falls outside of science has a magical or miraculous quality to it.

The more time we spend in the AL Flow State the more experiences we have that current, mainstream scientific models cannot explain, and the more these experiences are normalized for us. They become our new reality. Some of my favorite clients to work with are the ones who are naturally skeptical, logical, and grounded in their current belief system, yet still willing to entertain and fully engage in the Aligned Living practices. For these clients the only thing that changes their perspective is firsthand experience.

This describes my client Eddie to a T. The first time we worked together, he showed up with a skeptical curiosity. As we started the visualizations he shared, "That is interesting. There is kind of this tingly thing happening in my head. Very bizarre." I replied, "Yes, that is you starting to entrain with your own energy field. When we move our awareness from the external to the internal it becomes very quiet and we get to interact with and influence our own energy field." Eddie said, "Okay, interesting."

Over the next couple of sessions, Eddie was learning to stay in his sovereign and the AL Flow State. His first two major observations were how much authority he was instantly carrying and how much gratitude was coming back to him from others. This was true both at work and at home. When Eddie first came to see me, he was entertaining the idea of leaving his current place of employment. He was frustrated by his work environment and coworkers. By the third session, Eddie had discovered how much influence he had on his surroundings by staying in his alignment. The people around him were behaving differently and treating him with a new level of respect and gratitude. He saw it as a game.

He told me, "People around me say or do things that used to trigger me and spin me up. Now I see it like we are each planets and have our own gravitational fields. If we entrain with our own, we are drawn into our own alignment and the AL Flow State. If we pop out and entrain with others, their gravity pulls us into their world. It is like a game I play now. I keep choosing my own gravity over others, or if I slip and choose theirs, I realize it and come back to my own." At the end of the third session Eddie shared, "All this stuff used to sound crazy to me. Then it started to feel like magic. Now it just feels normal, like it is just how things are." Eddie was able to ground into this work, and what at first felt like magical thinking became more ordinary in his mind. His reality shifted. It wasn't magic, it was just how it is. When Eddie shared his short flirtation with magical thinking with me, I realized it was important to address in this book.

I have seen a strong, direct, positive correlation between a client's attachment to magical thinking and how often they lose track of their role in the shifts they are experiencing. This becomes a bigger problem when they are confronted with their plans hitting resistance and not coming together as quickly or in the manner they had hoped. Those prone to magical thinking are likely to look outside of themselves for a magical solution to appear and save them. They forget that they are the ones bringing the "magic" through their EMF by staying aligned and creating from that place of flow.

Jimmy is an incredibly dedicated and hardworking salesperson. At the same time, when his plans start to go sideways, he is prone to disengage from them and ask for divine intervention. Whether we believe in divine intervention or not is less relevant here than us staying engaged with what we are creating and holding our alignment. Even if you have complete faith in the divine, you still need to show up and do your part. When Jimmy would feel the discomfort of one of his deals falling apart, he often left his alignment and started seeking a magical solution. His thinking moved into attempting to use the AL Flow State to create a new opportunity or magical solution to the problem rather than staying aligned and inviting the problem into his alignment. At this point, his intuition and emotions would become entangled in each other, and he'd be drawn into a seemingly perfect solution that in reality would not work. He had tricked himself into thinking he was aligned. We can't stay aligned while simultaneously trying to avoid something.

Let me share Jimmy's latest bout with magical thinking as an example to give this concept some real-life context. Jimmy had been working hard to pull a deal together for months. A couple days before he had his client scheduled to sign their contract, Jimmy received a call from the client's financing company. The financing had fallen through. This put Jimmy into a panic; he left his alignment and moved into magical thinking. He completely forgot the role his own alignment and EMF were playing in creating the opportunity. He was thrilled when a young man who was out making cold calls walked into his office. Jimmy thought this young man was the answer to his problem. He was a loan officer. It felt like magic. Despite the fact that Jimmy was about to call another loan officer he knew and trusted, he dropped that plan the moment this new magical solution appeared in front of him. He gave his client's information to his new savior and felt like he had been rescued by the universe. A few minutes later he received a call from a potential client who was excited about having Jimmy help them out with some big purchases they had planned. He was so excited by all this divine intervention that he decided this was where he should put his energy. He shifted his full focus into this new opportunity and the old deal he had worked so hard to create would either come through or not.

The next day the new client had fizzled out and he had not heard from his new miracle loan officer. Jimmy realized he had forgotten that his alignment and the AL Flow State were the "magical" ingredients that made it all work in the first place. He had stopped bringing his "magic" and tried to defer his responsibility to a higher power. Luckily, it wasn't too late. Jimmy moved back into his sovereignty and the AL Flow State. He is a very spiritual person and decided to work *with* the divine support rather than removing himself from the equation and deferring his responsibility to a higher power, as he had done the day before. Jimmy got in touch with the loan officer he already knew and trusted and pulled the deal back together.

If a surgeon is losing their patient, they don't stop the surgery and pray for a miracle no matter how dedicated they are to the divine. They may see themselves as a tool of the divine and realize the only way their patient is going to be saved is through the surgeon's guided actions. They must stay fully present and engaged. This is true for whatever we are doing in life. We are creating these things ourselves. Whether your perspective includes the divine or not, you are still required to fully show up in your alignment in order to create the best possible outcome.

It is not uncommon for us to have incredible synchronicities when we are aligned. When we experience these moments, it is also a time for us to move into discernment rather than diving into magical thinking. When we stop and check in with our alignment and then utilize the Aligned Perspective technique, we receive instant clarity. Is this new opportunity the right action? Is this my intuition steering me into a disastrous situation so I can learn the value of discernment?

CHAPTER TWENTY-ONE

INFLUENCE

We perceive and are affected by changes too subtle to be described.

—Henry David Thoreau
*Early Spring in Massachusetts: From the
Journal of Henry D. Thoreau*

Today we are beginning to see old paradigm business leaders who operated out of fear and instilled that same fear in their employees losing their influence. They are operating in an outdated paradigm. What is emerging is a far more aligned and effective trend. These modern influential business leaders have a new set of traits in common. They are still authoritative, persistent, committed to a clear goal, and confident in themselves and their abilities, but they are also likable, authentic, high in integrity, helpful, innovative, passionate, trustworthy, courageous, and empowering. When we embody these traits, we naturally emerge into leadership and influence.

The Aligned Living work that we do sets us up for massive growth in each of these categories. Confidence is often the first trait to grow. When we are entrained externally, our confidence tends to fluctuate rapidly depending on who we are around and the situation we are embedded in. This keeps us from trusting our own ability to show up in our power. In some situations we can access it, and in others we struggle to find it. How can we be confident in ourselves if we can't count on an internal consistency? Trust is built with ourselves in the same way we build it with others. We all have people in our lives that have a bit of a wild card energy to them. We never know which aspect of themselves is going to show up each time we interact with them. We may like them (or not), but we definitely won't trust them to show up how we need them to. For those of us that are entrained externally we have a similar relationship with ourselves. Obviously this is true to varying degrees, but it is always a factor. When we shift to entraining internally and aligning with the AL Flow State we immediately start experiencing an internal consistency. The interference of outer influence dies down and we receive the clarity of who we are. As we commit to staying internal and aligned, this consistency teaches us to trust ourselves and results in a palpable shift in our confidence. We can count on ourselves and that internal truth is reflected externally in all areas of our lives.

As people experience us consistently showing up at our best, their trust in us grows. They can feel our stability and at some level know we are entrained internally. This is when we begin moving from influenced to influencer. This naturally progresses into us taking on a more authoritative role. We are seeing that we can trust ourselves, and now the people around us are reflecting that truth back to us. We are being asked to lead, and being the leader requires us to embrace and develop our ability to be authoritative. We are not talking about becoming dogmatic in our authority. Dogmatic leaders are usually coming from a place of fear, feeling as if things are out of control and they need to pull it all together. They are responding to a threat. When our authority is coming from an internal alignment, we already feel in control and know that our stability is contagious if we maintain it. The moment we move into a meddling role and try to make people follow us, we engage in a battle and the threat appears. When we stay in the AL Flow State, external threats tend to derail themselves. When two people set out to lead a group and one is in alignment while the other is operating from a place of fear and domination, it is obvious to everybody involved.

Gage had just started working a sales position in a small company that had been operating for four years. There was a team of four salespeople in addition to the owner, who was very involved in the day-to-day operations. Gage is a creative and dynamic guy. He loves to have an influence and create positive change. In past jobs, he had found himself triggering coworkers with his powerful presence, influence, and innovative ideas. Wherever he worked, he tended to upset the status quo. Gage had also been the definition of a Meddler. He was externally entrained and strong-willed. Through his work with Aligned Living, Gage understood this about himself. In fact, he had taken this sales job with a new company in order to start with a clean slate. He felt like he had a reputation of being difficult and had engaged in too many battles with his former coworkers. Rather than trying to shift his relationships, he decided to create new ones in a fresh setting.

Gage's first couple of weeks with his new company started out well. He was enjoying having a positive rapport with his coworkers and boss. He laughed to himself as he identified the personality traits in them that he knew he would have triggered in the past. But that hadn't been happening this time. By the third week, Gage started to get a bit nervous. His coworker Andy had been with the company for several years. She was somebody he would have immediately triggered in the past. Andy had a few patterns that showed up to Gage as red flags. She would often offer ideas in the morning sales meetings, but people seldom took them. It wasn't that they were necessarily bad ideas, it was more the way in which they were presented. Andy carried a lot of anger and felt wounded about not being heard. The energy around her ideas tended to turn everybody off of them. She felt unstable, and the rest of the team tried not to engage much beyond pleasantries with her.

The team was excited to have the new, dynamic energy Gage brought. His ideas were quickly accepted and implemented. In the first two weeks, he had already made a big impact on the work place and his influence could be seen in almost every area of operations. Gage was uncomfortably watching Andy be triggered by his success. He could tell that he was having the effect on the office that Andy had been trying to have for years. She had been in quiet opposition to Gage. Andy had convinced herself that the reason nobody was taking her ideas was because Gage was convincing them to take his. Andy began attempting to quietly build a case against Gage and subtly turn their coworkers against him. The moment Gage started to sense this happening, his old alarms went off. He began second-guessing all of the work he had been doing to stay internal and in the AL Flow State. He braced himself for the attack he knew was coming.

Sure enough, the next day Andy was visibly angry and glared at Gage throughout the day. Her anger seemed to grow, and by midafternoon Andy boiled over. She had taken advantage of the fact that she and Gage were the only ones in the office. Everybody else was out on calls. As Gage hung up from a phone call, he looked up to see Andy standing over him. She let loose in a tirade of accusations about how he was trying to take over the place and push her out of the way. For just a moment, Gage was triggered back into his old operating system. He stood up and started to return the anger and accusations. As the words started to come out of his mouth he felt himself transform into something he thought he had moved beyond. He realized he was completely entrained externally with Andy's rage. He felt it running through his body. He paused at his realization and reclaimed his sovereignty. He could feel himself move back into center and regain his composure and power. He simply responded with, "I'm sorry you feel that way. My intention is to help the company, not diminish your ideas."

Gage then sat back down and tried to go back to work. Andy was not interested in letting him off that easy. Much of the wind had gone out of her sails, but she wasn't about to give up. Andy continued laying into Gage about how he had changed everything since he got there and how hard it was making it for her to do her job. At this point Gage was starting to feel the influence he was having by staying aligned. He connected even deeper with the flow of his EMF and his spine, then said, "I'm sorry you are having a tough time with the changes. You should probably bring this up with the owner since he is the one that put my ideas into action. I can see you're angry, but I really don't know what else to say about it." Gage then turned around, and Andy stomped off. He was hoping he hadn't just done himself in by sending Andy to talk to the owner. He decided to do some damage control. He took a minute to make sure he was completely in the AL Flow State, and then calmly gave the owner a call. Gage explained his concerns to the owner and how he had redirected Andy to talk to him. Gage expressed that he understood why the changes were so upsetting to Andy, but wasn't sure how to support her. The owner said he would take care of it and assured Gage that it was not his problem to solve.

The rest of the team noticed the intense anger and blame coming from Andy. They had never seen her so upset before. The team also noticed how Gage didn't shift at all. Seeing Gage's consistency brought in a whole new level of trust for him. At the same time, Andy was quickly eroding the small amount of respect and trust she had built with her colleagues. Gage realized that just a few months ago he would have responded to the "threat" completely differently. He would have kept his entrainment with

Andy's anger and gone to battle. He would have shown an ugly side of himself and invited in future conflicts with the rest of the team. It took Andy about a month to let go of the battle she was trying to start with Gage. This was all amazing to Gage, as the outcome was different than anything he had experienced in the past, but the topper happened about six months later. Andy started coming to Gage for ideas and advice. She had accepted and begun to trust his authority and intention.

The shifts that Gage made and the results he created are quite typical of our clients. When he chose to stay aligned in the face of old triggers, he broke an old pattern. This was a significant turning point. Gage's new trust in himself now allows him to walk into situations that used to feel dangerous and know that there really is no threat. When we trust ourselves to not become reactive but to hold our alignment, we start to feel compassion for those who used to trigger us. We maintain our authenticity and integrity and show ourselves to be helpful, consistent, and trustworthy. We are far more likable, and even though we don't perceive what we are walking into as a threat, we do still show up to others as courageous and empowering through our example.

As we learn to live each day in the AL Flow State, we maintain a clarity of purpose and decisiveness and we know what is and is not in resonance with us. It is evident to ourselves as well as to those around us that we are clear about our goals and are persistent in pursuing them. We show up fully every day radiating our passion and confidence. This alignment heightens our awareness as we maintain continuous access to our intuition and the innovation it provides. Living in the AL Flow State, by its very nature, will move you from being influenced to influencer.

CHAPTER TWENTY-TWO

PARADOXICAL TRAITS

The curious paradox is that when I accept myself just as I am, then I can change.

—Carl R. Rogers
The Carl Rogers Reader

We each have a tendency to overuse our greatest strengths. We also tend to carry an identifiable level of avoidance of the opposite or paradoxical trait. For example, if you have found great success in your ability to schmooze and bring people on board with your ideas through diplomacy, you are less likely to utilize the paradoxical trait of being candid or direct. As a result, you limit your ability to be influential in situations that call for directness. When we try to use traits outside of our comfort zone, it is usually emotionally driven and ineffective. When our emotions surface, our authority is instantly eroded, and of course authority is a key element in being influential. Developing our weaker paradoxical traits creates exponential growth in our ability to be effective, flexible, confident, and influential. This is usually all happening outside of our own awareness. It is amazing how fast we can shift when we finally see within ourselves what is often obvious to the people around us.

A while back, my good friend and colleague Bob Petrello introduced me to Harrison Assessments and their "Paradox Technology." He has used Harrison Assessments in his executive coaching business for many years. Their inventories offer an abundance of information and need to be provided by a certified Harrison trained partner. The paradoxical traits are a major key to their effectiveness. The moment I was introduced to it, I saw the substantial value Harrison provides. I trained with Harrison, completed my certification, and now use their system with all of my business clients. It provides a grounded baseline to start from and deep insight into what has been driving old patterns.

Paradoxical traits are two traits that at first appear to be contradictory to each other but in truth are not. In fact, the way we work with the two paradoxical traits indicates our strength or weakness in a third connected skill set. Let's look at an example using what Harrison Assessments calls "decision approach," which it identifies as a combination of your tendencies to be "analytical" and/or "intuitive." Given the nature of my work, a good portion of my clients view themselves as intuitive. They see it as a powerful skill, and many of them turn to their intuition for guidance over being analytical. Initially, I hear them describe how analysis bogs people down and pulls them out of flow. Of course there is some truth in that statement, but avoiding analysis seldom creates a positive result. This avoidance is also one of the reasons I see people make the same mistakes over and over again, creating the same sorts of challenges in their work and personal lives.

Harrison Assessments uses four quadrants to classify your decision approach:

1) "Disinterested in Decisions," low scores in both "Analytical" and "Intuitive"

2) "Laser Logical," high score in "Analytical" and low score in "Intuitive"

3) "Non-Logical," low score in "Analytical" and high score in "Intuitive"

4) "Logical Intuition," high scores in both "Analytical" and "Intuitive"

The fourth quadrant, "Logical Intuition" is the decision-making approach that is the most effective. We can only operate from that place if we are willing to value both analysis and intuition. The similarity between quadrant four paradoxical traits and the AL Flow State are unmistakable. They are both an aligned balancing place between seemingly contradictory ways of being. They are like the thriving brackish ecosystem of an estuary that can only be created by the convergence of fresh and salt water. The AL Flow State is the balancing place where ordinary and non-ordinary reality converge, and the "Logical Intuition Decision Approach" is the balancing place between "Analytical" and "Intuitive" decision-making. This is all about balance and why many of the most successful people we know can seem so contradictory in nature.

When I first start working with clients that are "Non-Logical" quadrant decision makers I ask them two questions. "Why do you operate in this way?" and "How is that working out for you?" Being intuitively driven, the majority of these clients have simply followed their natural tendency to be intuitive, seldom analyzing how that was working out for them. Analysis often feels threatening to them, but few of these clients have stopped to consider if avoiding analysis was really helping them. Ironically, they had not analyzed the challenges they were creating for themselves through over reliance on their intuition. Many of these clients had not even realized they were avoiding analysis. After these first two questions, I ask a third question, "Would you rather be more nonlogical in your decision-making or more logical intuition based?" Of course, the answer is almost always logical intuition.

I was working with James, an extremely intelligent and powerful young man who was always on the verge of huge successes. Yet things often went sideways at the last minute for him. James's frustration with being so close to success only to have it flop is what brought him to see me. He scored eight out of ten on "Intuitive" and three out of ten on "Analytical," putting James soundly in the "Non-Logical" quadrant. This didn't look pretty on the graph Harrison provided, particularly with the big red circle that showed up in the "Laser Logical" quadrant. You earn a red circle whenever your paradoxical traits have a three point or greater gap between them. A three and an eight definitely qualified. What this indicated is that under pressure, James would abandon his intuition and make a sudden and obvious jump to being "Laser Logical." It was so obvious, in fact, that people could easily see it. Talk about undermining your own authority! Imagine having your salesperson being relaxed, confident, and easy to work with and then, as the deal started to come together, move into a whole different way of being. James's tightening up had often derailed him.

James shared that the household he grew up in was extremely logically minded. Anything that was not based on sound analysis was considered foolhardy. James also had a strong sense of self and would rebel from controlling situations. He was naturally intuitive and felt like the values of his household devalued him. This created an emotionally charged rebellion of abandoning logic for intuition. The realization struck James all at once—his rebellion was a form of control his parents still had over him. This brought him back into balance. He essentially rebelled against his former rebellion. Analysis stopped feeling like something trying to control him. He started using it as a synergistic tool in combination to his intuition. James realized his aligned state for

"Decision Approach" was "Logical Intuition." This shift translated into more trusting clients and bigger paychecks within a handful of weeks.

The Harrison Assessments identified a different primary challenge for my client Cindy. Her challenge was in "Driving," which refers to how you motivate people to do their work. Harrison Assessments examines the paradoxical traits of "Enforcing" (policing rules) and "Warmth / Empathy." The four quadrants are:

1) "Cool Permissiveness," low "Enforcing" and low "Warmth / Empathy" scores
2) "Harsh," high "Enforcing" and low "Warmth / Empathy" scores
3) "Permissive," low "Enforcing" and high "Warmth / Empathy" scores
4) "Compassionate Enforcing," high "Enforcing" and high "Warmth / Empathy" scores

Cindy scored fives in both "Enforcing" and "Warmth / Empathy." This placed her precisely in the center where all four quadrants converge. This indicated that Cindy was operating in each of the four quadrants. She would shift how she showed up depending on the situation. Initially this may sound positive, since her flexibility could ostensibly allow her to navigate whatever the situation called for. Unfortunately, shifting her behavior between quadrants was far more emotionally driven than analytical. This meant that her coworkers and direct reports didn't know how Cindy was going to react in any given situation. They didn't have a lot of trust for her because they didn't know what to expect. It had never occurred to Cindy that her behavior was fluctuating that much. She was aware of the lack of trust from her coworkers, but didn't connect it to her unpredictability.

Cindy's solution to not being trusted became quite simple. She had to be a little bit more fully committed to being both "Enforcing" and exercising her "Warmth / Empathy" traits. These small steps netted huge gains in her working relationships, particularly in her ability to motivate her direct reports.

As we live in the AL Flow State, we see so many of our triggers lose their potency. At that point, many of our actions around paradoxical traits are more about habit than old emotional reactions. We tend to keep doing what we have always done if we are not aware and intentional about our actions. Bringing our paradoxical traits into our awareness fast-tracks our growth process. With the trigger gone, changing our behavior is something we just choose to do. James embraced his logical side and laughed that it had taken him over thirty-five years to recognize it as a support. Cindy realized that in the past she was afraid people would be upset with her if she didn't slightly mute herself. The moment she realized that what she had thought was the solution was actually creating the problem, she joyfully stepped forward.

Harrison Assessments' "Paradox Technology" has proven to be a powerful tool to combine with the Aligned Living techniques. We use it in our coaching programs. As you can see, it assists clients in seeing their blind spots. I recommend you invest in this assessment, whether through Aligned Living or by finding another Harrison partner you trust.

CHAPTER TWENTY-THREE

EMBODYING YOUR NEXT LEVEL OF SELF

Most people only live for their image, that is why some have a void, because they are so busy projecting themselves as this or that, dedicating their lives to actualize a concept of what they should be like rather than to actualize their ever-growing potentiality as a human being. Wasting, dissipating all their energy in projection and conjuring up of facade, rather than centering their energy on expanding and broadening their potential or expressing and relaying this unified energy for efficient communication, etc.

—Bruce Lee
Striking Thoughts: Bruce Lee's Wisdom for Daily Living

On our individual paths of self-development, we all move through a process of letting go of our more immature traits as we become aware that they no longer serve us. We outgrow old behavior and thought patterns and start to adopt new ones. The Aligned Living work fast tracks this process. Our awareness grows quickly as we spend more time in the AL Flow State. This is one of the areas where a coach's influence often makes our clients' growth even more exponential.

What follows are the stories of several clients' experiences as they matured into embodying their next levels of self. At Aligned Living we often refer to the younger, less developed parts of ourselves as our prince, princess, or knight role. Our goal is to move from these roles into the roles of kings and queens. As you read through these clients' experiences, many of you will relate to each of the stories regardless of gender. We each have parts of ourselves that are traditionally considered more "masculine" or "feminine," and each of these aspects of self goes through a maturing process. As you read each individual case, look for the parts of you that you see reflected in each client's story. It may seem funny to think of a masculine man's inner princess or a feminine woman's inner prince or knight, but trust me, we all have played these roles to greater or lesser degrees. Additionally, the immature and mature traits we discuss in each of these clients' stories is not unique to a male or female. I have seen both men and women struggle as well as thrive in each of the areas we are about to examine.

From Prince to King

I am, indeed, a king, because I know how to rule myself.
—Pietro Aretino
Fifteenth century satirist,
author of infamous *Lust Sonnets*

Before you can be a king, you must first be a prince. Not all princes become king, but all kings were once a prince. This is the tale of my client Stefan and his journey from prince to king. The "prince" runs around the kingdom telling everybody that someday he will be king. His self-worth comes from his potential for future accomplishments. He tends to focus on himself and his immediate emotional needs. It is not uncommon for his ego to get the best of him as he tries to prove his worthiness. His moods and EMF can change quickly, depending on what is happening in his immediate experience. As he entrains externally, he often operates as the influenced rather than the influencer. He tends to chase after opportunities rather than allowing them to come to him. There is no judgment in this. Each of these ways of being have shown up for every one of us on our journey to become king.

Stefan is a tall, good-looking, confident guy. He is the kind of person that you know is going places the moment you meet him—a prince ready to become a king. But his achievements were limited, and from time to time he would have moments of self-doubt, runaway ego, and self-indulgence. These "prince"-like traits kept him from his potential of becoming a king.

Stefan had been working on his inner growth for several years before coming to me and signing up for the Aligned Living Six Week Program. As we sat down in his first session and went through his Harrison Assessments report, the picture came together quickly for both of us. Stefan was extremely optimistic and always expected huge successes. He knew he was destined to be a king. So, he showed up every day expecting it to happen. This optimism continued despite the fact that he kept coming up short of his goals. He figured that if he just kept at it, his current reality would eventually catch up with his vision of himself as king. We continued to uncover Stefan's unconscious inner workings. He was so committed to his optimism that he hated to spend much time identifying potential pitfalls. One of the assignments I gave him throughout the week was to monitor himself and see if he tried to ignore any red flags that could indicate potential problems down the road. Over the course of the week, it started to become clear to Stefan how often he would do this. Once he identified his behavior in the present, he could see how this had allowed multiple deals to fall apart in the past. He started identifying those moments where so many different experiences he had in his life had moved out of alignment. He hadn't tried to correct the course of the situation because he was afraid of derailing it.

The prince hopes for the best outcome, but the king takes actions to create it. The king is not passive and optimistic; he is empowered, influential, and discerning. When he sees the alignment, the optimism follows. This was the root of why Stefan was still stuck in being a prince. He didn't feel comfortable dealing with the potential pitfalls. It felt safer to ignore them than to identify and take action on them. As Stefan learned to live in the AL Flow State, he couldn't help but take action. He had a responsibility to his kingdom and himself. He stopped worrying about upsetting people or derailing deals. He realized those deals were already being derailed as they moved out of alignment. The only way to potentially save them was identifying the pitfalls and taking actions to bring it all back into alignment. Stefan reflected on all the hours he put into deals that never had a real chance of closing. It became clear how he had optimistically duped himself.

Now one of Stefan's biggest priorities is to stay in the AL Flow State. He knows that from this place he can feel and quickly identify when one of his client relationships or potential deals is moving out of alignment. He doesn't hesitate to take action when he sees this happening. I worked with Stefan in many areas of his work life, but this was his initial block to stepping up to being a king. This ownership over his life brought in a new grounded confidence that others could see. People responded to this by recognizing and honoring his authority. As people's responses to Stefan were reflected back to him, it had a synergistic effect. He moved from optimistically expecting to become a king into already being one. Stefan's boss started inviting him to meetings with top tier clients. With a big smile on his face he told me, "These guys are all much older than I am and hugely accomplished, but they still listen to my ideas and use them. It feels amazing." I replied, "Of course they do Stefan, a king recognizes another king."

From Princess to Queen

Think like a queen. A queen is not afraid to fail. Failure is another stepping stone to greatness.

—Oprah Winfrey
Business Insider, Nov, 3, 2013

Like the prince and the king, every queen was once a princess, but not every princess becomes a queen. I can't tell you how many clients have come to me with the realization that they were embodying the princess at some level. They had mostly seen themselves as queens, but had been confronted with the harsh reality of how present the princess role was in their lives. Let me introduce you to Lilly. Lilly is a smart, talented, and capable woman in her thirties. She had an awareness of ways she worked with the princess role, but as she started her work with Aligned Living, Lilly became much more deeply aware of certain truths she couldn't ignore. She realized how much of her self-esteem was dependent on continuous attention from others. It was a habit she had developed early in her life.

For Lilly, when operating in her princess role, she influenced by becoming what others wanted her to be or expected from her. She was more interested in pleasing others by putting on a façade than in the reality of who she was. But she lived in constant fear because she knew the tools she used to get the attention she wanted were not sustainable. They had an expiration date. This date cast a shadow over her inner balance, and anxiety was almost always a byproduct. She had created a life where her welfare and lifestyle were dependent on being someone she wasn't. She believed that if she stopped appearing the way her benefactors wanted her to, they would redirect their attention to a new recipient. She lived in this prison cell of her own making, all the while posting it on social media from just the right angle, with the prison bars just out of the picture. She never set out to live her life this way, it was just the easiest path to her goals. She didn't trust herself and failed to see her true power, so she took the easy route.

At a very young age, Lilly was considered attractive and much admired as a result. This had a lot of payoffs, and like anybody else with a trait that works for them, she developed and overused it. Lilly found that the more she shifted herself to match who others wanted her to be, the more appealing they found her. She perceived her ability to make herself attractive to others as directly connected with keeping her personality flexible to the situation. If we look at this in the context of paradoxical traits, there are several traits we could plug in as paradoxical to her flexible personality. For this example we will use the trait of being authoritative. That means that for Lilly, whenever she would take on any kind of authoritative role, it would appear to her that it diminished her agreeableness and thus her attractiveness. This felt dangerous because she knew that by being flexible she could get what she wanted. In order to find power and influence through her authority she would have to risk letting go of her most reliable quality.

This was not a risk Lilly was willing to take until recently, when she realized she couldn't continue to sacrifice her true power for external validation and attention. She knew that embodying authority would take some time to pay off. This meant intentionally moving into a period of time where she would stop engaging in her princess energy and trust that she would learn to generate internal power by embracing her own sense of authority. Lilly found herself struggling with this trust and sliding back and forth in her ability to turn down external opportunities to validate herself in old ways and staying true to her commitment and internal power.

Within a month of this struggle, while fully committing to her Aligned Living practices, Lilly was able to stabilize, and to trust herself and the process. Lilly had combined her naturally flexible and pleasing nature with her authority to find her true presentation of self. She became empowered. People were still drawn to her, but whereas before it was as if they wanted her as an accessory. Now that she had embraced her authority, she became an empowered equal in their eyes. She was no longer diminishing her power; her appeal accentuated her authority, prompting people to look to her for guidance. Something had clicked. The next week when I saw Lilly, I almost didn't recognize her. She had stopped adjusting herself to be what she thought was appealing to the people around her. She seemed much taller and more confident. Lilly was internally entrained and radiating her true self. The Gift of Rejection and the Tractor Beam were fully engaged. She was embodying her queen energy.

If you are reading these personal accounts and feeling intense realizations of these stories reflecting a truth in your life, you are probably experiencing an invitation to leave your alignment and become fully entrained with this challenge. Take a couple of deep breaths, reset, and re-entrain with yourself. This is a perfect opportunity to work with the Aligned Perspective technique. Now that you are operating internally in your sovereign state and connecting with the AL Flow State, pay particular attention to connecting with your EMF running through the back of your brain, brain stem, and spine. Feel yourself grounding as you connect with the earth. Once you know you are fully entrained with your alignment, invite any areas of your life where you may be operating in the prince or princess realm into your centered space. Forget about any stories you think you already know. You are like a fly on the wall observing your own life. What shows up? As you observe yourself outside of judgment, connect with your compassionate self. Know that any past choices to connect with the prince or princess roles made sense at the time. Honor this truth and then ask: Where have I outgrown this role? Where is it appropriate for me to graduate into my king or queen energy? What does that look like? What will this change?

At this point most people fall into two mindsets. About half the people I work with have a sobering experience of, "Wow, this is going to change things, but I need to do it." and the other half are so focused on seizing their king or queen power that they are not in touch with what this will create in their lives. They wildly start running around planting explosive charges in every area of their life that smells the slightest hint of prince or princess. If this is you, before you detonate these charges, take a minute. From your inner balance, ask both your intuitive and analytical self to guide you into the right actions. What will happen if you set off all those charges at once? Both those experiencing sober realizations and the ones planning a new career as a munitions expert will be best served by moving forward in a place of balance. You have operated for years with the prince and/or princess roles present in your life. Your new awareness has forced your brain into reidentifying as a huge threat what it once embraced as a powerful gift. Don't be fooled by your brain's sudden urgency. What would the queen do? What would the king do? She or he would take logical, strategic steps forward to regain their power, while the princess or prince would throw a fit and break things. Your first step in becoming the queen or king is to handle this realization as the queen or king, solid, grounded, logical, intuitive and powerful. Be patient with yourself and stay aligned.

From Knight to King or Queen

Self-sacrifice which denies common sense is not a virtue. It's a spiritual dissipation.

—Margaret Deland
The Rising Tide

The knight is not born into royalty. In fact, the knight is born into service to all, including to royalty. Knights often position themselves next to royalty and champion their causes, as well as those of the people who can't champion their own causes. The knight's identity is connected with service to others and putting their own needs aside. The few knights who become royalty earn every step of their long path. They don't even know it is the path they are on until they have almost completed their need to walk it. Knights generally take many laps that follow these predictable steps, initiating their cycle with selfless service, giving far more than can ever be requited. They do this with joy, purpose, and no sense of where it is headed. Inevitably the knight loses their internal drive in this imbalanced process. Feelings of resentment, being taken advantage of, and often betrayal start to show up, revealing once more how unsustainable this selflessness is. The cycle then moves into a period of withdrawal, as the knight attempts to serve their own needs over others. This never lasts long, since the knight is hardwired to serve others. They complete their cycle by reopening their channel of selfless giving and then proceeding to take another lap. The knight has a unique mixture of self-admiration while at the same time not being able to see their worth beyond service to others. The primary way they sustain their self-admiration is through service, thus driving them to repeat their cycle over and over again.

Something interesting happens when the knight accesses their sovereignty. For many, they realize for the first time they are truly separate from others. There has always been a connection they have felt with others, making the needs of who they feel in service to nearly indistinguishable from their own. They have an innate drive to take action, to put the needs of those they are in service to above their own—to follow the knight's code. Sovereignty and the AL Flow State breaks this illusion. They experience a period where their old motivators stop feeding them. They usually continue giving out of habit and are surprised when the giving feels empty and out of alignment. They must deliberately find a new food source—a new way to find meaning in their life.

Knights generally have many unwritten agreements with those they have been serving. They most likely have a long list of people who have been depending on their endless giving and self-sacrifice. Knights have a responsibility to back out of these agreements gracefully and without resentment. They must remember they were willing partners in the imbalanced relationships they were a part of. I am not advocating for a lengthy sentence of continued self-sacrifice but rather responsibly excusing yourself from the agreement rather than simply hitting the eject button.

Curtis felt he was sitting amongst royalty. How had he ended up in this mastermind group with all these kings? (A mastermind group is usually a peer-to-peer mentoring group with the intention of helping each member solve problems with the assistance of the collective members.) They were all so accomplished. What was his role in all of this? Well, he was the knight and kings do tend to attract knights. When in the AL Flow State, Curtis was feeling differently about himself, but was not yet aware of how he was appearing differently to others. Curtis had always been eager to be of service to the kings. It was his natural inclination. A few weeks into our work together he found this inclination feeling quite different to him.

In the middle of the mastermind group meeting one of the kings, in fact the leader of the kings, asked Curtis to take on some logistical responsibilities for the group. Much to Curtis's surprise, as well as the kings', he turned down the request. It felt out of alignment to him. His perspective of himself had changed. He wasn't there to serve the kings anymore, he was there to be a king. When our self-concept changes, we treat ourselves differently, like we have teleported from one perspective about ourselves into an entirely different and much more empowered one. It is important for us to remember that this change happened internally. The people around us are going to be surprised by how differently we show up and interact. We promote ourselves without the permission of others, and our choices force changes in our relationships.

The more we can be aware of this happening the more gracefully we can change. This is not easy to track, since we are operating from a place of new instincts. There is a big swing in behavior when we move from knight to king. Pushback is fairly inevitable. Luckily, knights are brave and practiced at walking forward into precarious situations. The difference here is that now they are doing it for themselves instead of just for others. The self-sacrifice is no longer enticing. Curtis is currently working through this process as he renegotiates all of his relationships. It's good to be king.

Becoming a king or queen is not a onetime achievement. Just like living in the AL Flow State, it takes a full commitment. Don't be surprised to find yourself slipping back into walking and talking like a prince, princess, or knight. When this happens, own it like a king or queen. Step into your full awareness, set things straight, own your actions, and realign.

CHAPTER TWENTY-FOUR

TEAM FLOW

If I told you that you weren't going home until we win—
what would you do differently?

—Stanley McChrystal
Team of Teams: New Rules of
Engagement for a Complex World

Almost every business professional is required to work, at least to some degree, with groups and teams. Most of us have experienced teams comprised of superstars that just couldn't seem to align their visions, and as a result little was accomplished. You also may have experienced teams where everybody worked together to create a synergy that none of the members could have generated separately. When team leaders are in the AL Flow State, they tend to entrain the rest of the team to move into flow as well. When leaders control their inner world and hold it stable, this stability is transferred to the team through their EMFs. The team members entrain with the leader, and their alignment becomes contagious in a very positive way. The team then benefits from the shifts the AL Flow State creates: diminished egos, more innovative and outside of the box thinking, and greater clarity and decisiveness. The team moves in connection with one another.

We have all worked with that leader whose mere presence inspires each team member to step into their best. The moment this leader shows up and engages their energy, the team comes together in a synergistic way. The members work together with a common goal. They want to show the leader what they are capable of, not just as individuals, but first and foremost as a team. These leaders make a world of difference, but unfortunately, they are also hard to come by. Let's look at a three different types of leaders and what they create. Few leaders fall into just one category. Most fall somewhere on a continuum between the Emotional Egoic Leader and the AL Flow State Leader. Of course, we are striving to be the AL Flow State Leaders.

The Emotional Egoic Leader

Unfortunately, the most common leader is the Emotional Egoic Leader. This leader operates in fear of failure. When they feel the pressure to perform, they entrain with that pressure and pass it directly onto their team. Not only does this type of leader not shelter their team members from the storm, they add on to it. This leader is quick to blame and celebrate individuals. They have their favorite and least favorite team members, and the whole team knows who these individuals are. The Emotional Egoic Leader is entrained externally, and their EMF is very unstable. Their emotional reactions are contagious to their team. They create an unsafe feeling where members of the team become competitive with each other while at the same time being afraid to take risks. They know taking a risk will either result in them being a hero or a scapegoat. This also inspires members to periodically take desperate, impulsive, and often unethical risks in an attempt to recuperate from past poor performances or to become the favorite.

Every day is a new day, and yesterday's accomplishments are quickly forgotten. This leader wants to know what you are doing for them today. Therefore their favorite and least favorite team member could switch places in an afternoon. There is no stability. Each of these aspects of the Emotional Egoic Leader's team is a direct reflection of the leader's unstable internal state and EMF. When pressure hits, being on a team like this can feel like trying to sail a ship through a storm where the captain and each crew member is only focusing on trying to save themselves. They lose track of the greater truth that the team needs to work together to survive. These teams have a lot of turnover, and this is often blamed on the individual's inability to perform.

The Cash Cow Leader

The Cash Cow Leader has a system figured out. They are entrained internally and are calm, stable, and grounded. This levelheaded energy is contagious to their team. Cash Cow Leaders tend to shelter their team members from the added pressure to perform coming from higher-ups. Each member has a specific role, and they have been trained to do it well. They know they are each an important cog in the machine. Every member is treated with the same level of respect and understands that the machine only works if each individual is doing their job. The Cash Cow Leader takes great pride in their ability to train their team members to perform their individual roles. As much as this leader values each team member, they also know they can train a replacement that will perform at about the same level. This team seldom has superstars or scapegoats. They succeed as a unit. The only records this team generally sets are for consistent and good quality performance. The Cash Cow Leader's team feels safe; it lacks inspiration, but offers stability.

The AL Flow State Leader

The AL Flow State Leader is entrained internally and aligned. They bring their best every day, they know what this looks and feels like, and they are consistent in it. They operate at the top of their game, and it is contagious. Everybody around them is inspired to bring their best and feels driven to demonstrate their excellence to their AL Flow State Leader. This demonstration looks markedly different than the brown nosing and cut throat behavior on the Emotional Egoic Leader's team. The team members know that type of behavior would not be tolerated here. The AL Flow State Leader does not operate from a place of ego. Instead, they operate from a place of showing up fully. When we give our best with our ego in the back seat, we feel the drive to support each other. We come together with the same goal, each operating at the top of our game, and synergy is the result.

These different types of leadership are easy to identify in coaches for athletic teams. Sports are a great arena to illustrate what each of these types of leaders bring out in their teams. We get to see how the team members respond to the leadership styles as individuals as well as a collective group. This all plays out in a small window of time and with an audience. My teenage daughter plays on a club sports team with three different coaches. The club has multiple teams, so the coaches rotate which team they coach for different games. Each of these coaches happen to perfectly personify these three types of leaders. Particularly in this age group, the influence of the coaches translates directly into how the individual players and team as a whole performs.

When Anna, the Emotional Egoic coach is in charge, there is little team cohesiveness. The players begin the game with each of them trying to be the star. Anna's energy is very excitable and gets the girls riled up. They play aggressively but in an unorganized manner. The game continues in this way unless the team starts to fall behind. At this point Coach Anna will pick out scapegoats and start to disengage from the team. But when they are winning it is her team and her heroes. The moment they start to lose, the pressure is put on individuals and Anna becomes angry and takes little to no responsibility in the process. Once the team starts to fall behind, they slowly unravel and tend to lose by a pretty big margin. Overall, their play is rather unpredictable, since under Anna's guidance they become emotionally and egoically reactive. They are just as likely to beat a more skilled team as they are to lose to lesser team.

When Danny, the Cash Cow coach, is in charge, the team really comes together as a unit. The players are much more aware of their responsibility to the team. Everybody plays hard and at a grounded, steady pace. Danny stays engaged with the team in the same manner, regardless of how the game is going. The girls respond to their coach's even demeanor by matching it. The team ends up being far more successful under Danny than Anna. They are much more likely to win if they are the better team. However, they are also more likely to lose if they are the lesser team. There are very few surprises or standout performances on the team in the positive or in the negative. Under Danny's coaching, they tend to have close scoring games, often going into overtime. They lose about 70 percent of those games by a couple of points of margin. The team has a tough time finding that spark and excited, competitive drive to surge ahead. They keep their even pace and usually come up just short.

When Sharman, the AL Flow coach is in charge, every aspect of the girls play steps up. Like Danny, Sharman is grounded and fully engaged. This creates a safe feeling for each player and helps them come together as a team. In fact, Sharman shows up very much like Danny with a couple exceptions. Whereas Danny uses her stability as a safe place to settle into, Sharman uses it as a launch pad. She expects the girls to take risks when the opportunity shows up and to push themselves out of their comfort zone and to the top of their game. The players feel Sharman's support, and they respond. Their dynamic play is not emotional in nature like Coach Anna often brings out in them. Instead, it is determined and driven from a solid, even place.

It really is amazing to watch as the players each entrain with Sharman's grounded intensity and winning spirit. They have the best record by far under Sharman and win almost every one of their close games. In their final game of last season, Anna was coaching the team, and as has happened many times before, they were getting blown out. The game Sharman was coaching had ended, and she came over to assist Coach Anna with about ten minutes left until the final buzzer. The change in the team was instantaneous the moment Coach Sharman showed up. You would have thought they were different players. They visibly moved from feeling defeated to inspired. In those final minutes, they turned a blowout into a competitive game. Unfortunately, they didn't have enough time left on the clock to win, but they were shown a spark in themselves that they couldn't access under Coach Anna's emotional egoic leadership.

As a team leader, you have a responsibility to set the tone for your team. Remember the "Emerging Leader" experiment from chapter four? We looked at how the rest of the team entrained with the vital signs of the leader. When we aren't grounded and internally stable, then our team won't be either. They may even entrain with one of their team members instead of you. The good news is that when we are aligned in the AL Flow State we naturally move into the role of influencer. We are recognized as a leader that others want to follow, and they tend to do just that.

I encourage you to play in this realm and conduct some experiments. Even if you are not the team leader, you can still stabilize and inspire the team. You probably have a pretty clear idea of how different people in your work life respond to you. Some may find your ideas inspiring while others may discount what you share. Some are encouraging and some stifling. It is the nature of people and teams. Try being intentional about moving into sovereignty and the AL Flow State right before you interact with these people. Stay internal and aligned throughout the time you are with them, and observe how they respond to you and what you have to say. You may be surprised by what comes out of your mouth, how it sounds, as well as how it is received. I have heard from many clients that even their voices sound different. Experimenting with their ability to have influence and authority is often another turning point for clients. When they see the proof in action, it inspires them to raise their commitment to living in the AL Flow State. It is fascinating to experience how positively and powerfully you can be received.

You will also become an expert in identifying the role the emotions and egos of others, particularly of leaders, play into how they affect the team. You will watch people gain and lose authority and influence. You will watch those with authority and influence inspire others to greatness, or put their team into a tailspin. Once you identify the active variables in the equation, the AL Flow leaders will be easy to identify, as will the Emotional Egoic and Cash Cow leaders. This will serve you well as a team member and when you are in a position of choosing leaders, and particularly as you are shaping the type of leader you are becoming.

As we looked at back in chapter nine on ideal conditions for flow states, there is a lot we can do as leaders to set our teams up to enter flow. Take a second look at the four conditions identified by Dr. Mihalyi Csikszentmihalyi and the nine social conditions from Dr. Keith Sawyer's lists on page 61. You will notice the themes that run through these ideal conditions. The team needs to know, honor, and respect each other; be forward focused and work towards the same goals; have the individual skill sets to equitably contribute; and the tasks need to require enough effort without being overwhelming.

I recognize there is always the ideal, and then there is the practical. It will be easy to look at this list and find the reasons your team can't hit all of them. You will see the team members that break the flow and the ones that help create it. The habits are most likely already in place. As a leader, it is your job to gain the buy-in of the group and steer the members into an additive culture. I find it helpful to get clear about where your team is currently operating from and what your goal is. There is almost always a few initial shifts you can orchestrate that create big dividends. Then the fine-tuning takes more time, guidance, and patience.

Once we clearly see the blocks to team flow, it is tempting to feel an urgency to change them. It is easy to see the blocks as a threat and overreact. You have made a sudden shift in perspective and, in most cases, are about to change the rules for your team members. It is important that you provide the guidance around what needs to shift and why. Then allow your team time and support to adjust their thinking. This can only work if you provide the space for group flow to become the team's goal.

It is important to present this as an experiment. You can even make it a game. I recommend collecting some baseline data so the team can see the results you are all creating together. The more value the individuals see in the experiment, the more likely they are to buy in and create even bigger results. This is a perfect opportunity to utilize your new sense of authority and influence to pull the team together. Keep your alignment and resist the temptation to "push against the cage." In other words, allow the flow to happen, don't force it to happen. As each team member buys in, they will influence the others as well. Trust the process and the pace at which it needs to happen.

CHAPTER TWENTY-FIVE

THE TRAPPINGS OF SUCCESS

Success has ruin'd many a Man.

—Benjamin Franklin
Poor Richard's Almanack

I n life there is a temptation to put things into several categories—things I want to change, things I am willing to change,
and then the "don't touch" pile. The more success we have the
more likely we are to add to the don't touch pile. If we were to stay
in our old linear consciousness, this would make sense. Once we
move into the AL Flow State, we realize everything is connected
and the categories we created can actually be working against us.
As you have been spending time in the AL Flow State, you have
most likely felt things shifting in your world. Have you also felt
yourself attempting to pull certain aspects of your life out of the
equation? We have a tendency to choose the things that are dear-
est to our hearts or any area we are receiving a substantial benefit from. This can be personal relationships, employees, ideas,
ways we see ourselves, or aspects of our business, to give a few
examples.

Once you have achieved success in certain areas of your life
and are still enjoying those successes, it's hard to imagine not

protecting them by taking them out of the growth equation. Remember, the growth that comes from living in the AL Flow State is about releasing what is out of alignment and calling in what is in alignment. Think back to the Tractor Beam and the Gift of Rejection. It may be scary not to protect our "do not touch" pile, but the truth is that if something is in alignment, the work you are doing will actually protect it more than you ever could by shielding it. Just as true is that if something is out of alignment, this work will force it to adjust or not be part of your life anymore. Once we see this truth show up reliably and repeatedly in our lives, it reveals something else about our do not touch pile. It shows us if we really trust that everything in the pile is in alignment with us. If it is in resonance, that match in frequency will hold it together better than we ever could through our protective actions.

In order for us to fully move into and maintain the AL Flow State, we have to be willing to let everything in our lives readjust. This may just be subtle shifts or it may be more profound. But if we don't allow for the subtle shifts, the profound ones will seldom happen. I have seen this show up for many of my more accomplished clients. There is a tendency for them to feel they have certain areas of their lives figured out because of past successes. They are egoically attached to certain ideas and self-concepts. They claim to be all in (and believe they are) while at the same time being unwilling to let old ingrained ideas or ways they see themselves shift. This manifests in an array of frustrations in their life. They are creating from a place that is slightly out of alignment with their true selves.

This is a place where an outside perspective may be necessary to break the illusion. This is also why coaching is so valuable. Take a serious look at the feedback you have been receiving. Look at previous 360 reviews or whatever your company provides for feedback. Are there any areas you are resisting or discounting? If so, let go of knowing your truth and see what changes. Our egos can derail us from maintaining the AL Flow. When you are willing to let everything in your life be free game, a freedom shows up that allows your life to shift in miraculous and supportive ways.

A similar trap often shows up after reaching big goals through flow work. I have seen so many clients achieve the position they wanted, finally land that big sale or even accomplish a personal goal like a loving relationship, and then try to stop the train of growth. They are like, okay, this is my stop. I'm getting off here. Thanks for the ride. However if we try to abandon what got us there in the first place (living in the AL Flow State), we will struggle to maintain what we have created. Our EMF moves out of alignment, and we begin operating in old ways. Our old ways don't match what we created, and it starts to fall apart. Flow work is not about being a one-hit wonder, it is about life getting better and better and more and more in alignment.

My favorite analogy for this is the monkey trap. A simple, proven way to catch a monkey is to place an apple inside of a transparent jar. The opening to the jar needs to be just slightly larger than the apple. The monkey will approach the jar and see their prize inside. They will then reach into the jar to grab the apple. Once the monkey has their hand around the apple, they discover the opening to the jar isn't big enough to pull their hand back out without letting go of the apple. Since the monkey has the prize in their hand, they are unwilling to let go and become trapped. Even though they can't enjoy the apple, in their mind they still have it. They are so close to victory that there is no turning back. Sometimes we get so close to achieving our goals that we can see them right in front of us. We get locked in on the idea that since we are so close to the solution, we can't reassess the situation. Like the monkey, we decide if we let go of the apple we may lose it. In truth, holding on to the apple is what is keeping us from having it. We don't realize we can let go of the apple, flip the jar upside down, and let the apple roll out of the opening and right back into our hands.

It is so easy to decide that a success (i.e. having the apple in our hands) is off-limits and that if we attempt to adjust it we may lose it altogether. These types of successes become our "sacred cows." We don't need to protect our sacred cows. If they truly are sacred cows, they won't go anywhere. They may be subtly adjusted, but they will stick around. Of course, if we think something is a sacred cow but in actuality is not in resonance with us, it will fall apart. Then in time it will be replaced with a true sacred cow. This is the ultimate test of living fully. Would you rather hold on to an illusion of alignment or be willing to let it go so you can achieve a life of true alignment? Not everybody will answer this question in the same way. The important thing is to answer the question honestly. If you lie to yourself, you will be inviting in all sorts of discomfort.

CHAPTER TWENTY-SIX

DIET AND EXERCISE

The greatest wealth is health.

—A familiar adage

I decided to add a chapter about diet and exercise simply because it inevitably comes up for most of our Aligned Living clients. As our relationship with ourselves changes, so does the way we treat ourselves. I imagine a good portion of the people reading this book saw the title of this chapter and instantly felt like something was going to be asked of them— that I would pressure them to take better care of themselves through diet and exercise. I can ensure you this chapter is not about external pressure to make changes in self-care. The more time we spend in the AL Flow State, the more aware we become of what is and what is not supportive to us. This is just as true in relation to what is happening inside ourselves as it is to what is happening outside of us.

What this means is that if you commit to staying aligned, you will most likely become more sensitive to the unhealthy diet being consumed by the majority of the population. As you become a more finely tuned version of yourself, you will start requiring better fuel. Clients generally respond to this idea in several different ways. The first is total resistance. "I'm not going to become one of those high-maintenance, pain-in-the-butt people that special orders everything at restaurants." They consider specialized diets to be a weakness.

Let me ask you this, would you make fun of the person who pulled up to the gas pump in their Ferrari and insisted on only putting premium grade gas in their vehicle? Would you scoff at them if they told you there were some gas stations they wouldn't even go to because they didn't trust their gas? No, you would say, "Hey, if I had a Ferrari I would feel the same way." Well, when you maintain the AL Flow State your body becomes like a Ferrari. You can't put economy fuel in it and expect it to perform in the same way, because it won't and it will require a lot more maintenance. As you begin relating to your body in this way you will instinctively desire healthier food and more exercise. Allowing yourself to follow your instincts here will serve you well. If you resist these natural changes because they feel picky or needy, you are working against yourself. Trust what your body wants. If you are embarrassed by how people in your life may judge you as high-maintenance, you can simply reply, "Sure, I'm picky, my body is high-maintenance, much like a Ferrari!"

The second common way clients respond is by trying to force this change instead of listening to their body. Are you one of these people who is tempted to clear out your fridge and cabinets on day one and replace them with only what you believe is healthy? Are you somebody who can be overzealous and enthusiastically dive in head first? These intentions are wonderful; unfortunately, this is also the same group that is most likely to find themselves at the fast-food drive through later that afternoon. These changes are not about will power or forced change.

The third group of clients are the ones who put their attention on staying aligned and over time find their diet naturally shifting. Several months down the road, they look back and wonder how their diet and amount of exercise changed so much. Their intention was not to eat healthier, it was to stay aligned. From this place, change happens without the same struggles. Sure, you may be eating great and then see a chocolate cake at a party that looks fantastic and grab a piece. It may even taste fantastic, but later your body will let you know if that was a good idea or not. The stomachache that may follow is your body reminding you of how it needs to be treated.

When we allow for changes to happen without resisting them or forcing them, we do it from a place of alignment. We are cooperating with and supporting ourselves. At this point, I eat a gluten-free, plant-based, and alcohol-free diet. Believe me, this was never my intention. The first dietary shift for me was alcohol. I enjoyed drinking beer. It was part of my lifestyle and social connections. I even had a kegerator in my basement with microbrews on tap. What tasted great and felt good in my body at one point started tasting bad and feeling like poison to my system. I didn't quit drinking alcohol. I stopped wanting it. At the time I became a vegetarian, I loved eating meat and was even teaching a barbecue class. One day it just stopped looking appealing and my body didn't want it anymore. Overtime I have fine-tuned my diet to match what feels good. Note that it is not what I have been told is good, it is what feels good, and this will be slightly different for everyone.

Desire for exercise shows up in very much the same way. Cycling and running have been a constant part of my life, so this change looked different for me. What changed instead of the desire was the effortlessness of the exercise. I used to focus on overcoming the challenge of pushing myself, but now it is about thriving in the experience. This shift is difficult to articulate. Capturing the essence of what it's like to exercise in the AL Flow State is not easy. My stamina has reached new levels, and it feels like I am effortlessly accessing energy from a new reserve I didn't know existed.

The key to these shifts in diet and exercise is listening to our bodies, allowing the change to happen, and embracing the results. Working with a nutritional coach and/or personal trainer who understands your process can be a great idea, and has proven highly effective for many of my clients. It is up to you to recognize if you benefit from that type of support or thrive under your own direction and experimentation.

CHAPTER TWENTY-SEVEN

INTEGRATION

Events in one area of our lives cascade into every other area.

—Michael Hyatt
*Living Forward: A Proven Plan to Stop
Drifting and Get the Life You Want*

Whenever I work with clients, they see big changes and achievements with the goals we set. This is the delivery of what was promised, and it's of incredible value. Sometimes what is even more valuable, though, is how the Aligned Living work affects the rest of our lives. When we develop new perspectives, skill sets, and ways of interacting with the world, it changes everything. When we create changes in work relationships, we will also see shifts in personal relationships. When we become more influential at work, the same trait develops in our personal lives. The more we live in the AL Flow State, the more integrated all aspects of our lives become. We are more present, and everything shifts around us to reflect that. The majority of my clients become so excited about what they are creating in their personal lives that we end up dedicating a significant amount of each session to this arena.

As I have placed this chapter at the end of this book, I'm sure you already know what I am talking about. As you work through the changes you are creating, it can take a lot of faith in this process to maintain the trust to continue with it. You will be presented with people that are excited about your growth, people who are terrified by the changes you are making, and most often a mixture of both. When you are in the AL Flow State you will most likely feel comfortable with people's reactions to you. The moment you allow yourself to be triggered out of alignment, you will start second-guessing yourself and this work. You will begin entraining with the EMFs of those around you, which will result in you taking on their perspectives and moving into their consciousnesses. If you maintain an awareness during these experiences, you can recognize in the moment that you are simply trying on different states of consciousness and the perspective that goes with them. If you lose your awareness, then you will confuse other people's consciousnesses and perspectives as your own and begin operating and making decisions from that place. This is a trap that most people practicing Aligned Living have fallen into at one time or another. It is fairly inevitable. The question is, will you recognize what you are doing and bring yourself back into your alignment?

There will be people in your life that you will feel the need to explain yourself to, particularly family members and close friends. These are the people whose support you would love to have throughout this process but who are often not in a place to understand what you are initiating in your life. This requires a great deal of discernment in what to share. Obviously, what you experience in the AL Flow State can sound outrageous to those who have not experienced it. If you are not sure how your explanation will be received, it is often more effective to simply demonstrate the validity of what you are doing by creating powerful shifts in your life. Living in your alignment is your most powerful tool. As you do this, people will notice. It is quite common for clients to share with me experiences of being pulled aside by others and asked, "What are you doing? What is going on in your life?" People often want to assume something has changed in your external world that explains why you seem so different. Once they realize it is something new you are doing with your internal world, they want to know that secret as well.

Aligned Living work can be explained at many different levels. What level of explanation matches the conversation, the setting, and the openness of the other party or parties involved? It can be as simple as, "I have a new meditation practice that helps me in many areas of my life." Or maybe, "I never realized how affected I was by everybody else around me. I have a new meditation practice that has helped me separate from all that and get more in touch with myself." You will come across people you can share openly with, and it may surprise you who that is. The question to ask yourself in deciding what to share is this: Is what I'm sharing supporting myself and the other parties in the conversation or is it serving some other impulse or desire?

CHAPTER TWENTY-EIGHT

LIVING IN FLOW

The sky is not the limit ... I am

—T. F. Hodge

*From Within I Rise: Spiritual Triumph over Death and
Conscious Encounters with "The Divine Presence"*

Once you have accessed the AL Flow State, life will never be quite the same. There will be an instant foundational shift and recognition of how much power we each carry to create and influence our life experiences. The degree to which we seize this power varies considerably from one individual to the next. This chapter is about self-commitment and a plan forward. We looked at a daily practice that allows us to keep growing and developing in all areas of our lives. We have also focused on turning this practice into a habit. The goal is for the AL Flow State to be the place you go when under stress, and to learn to override the natural tendency to revert back to your old, ineffective, and reactionary coping mechanisms. We rewire our systems to seek out the AL Flow.

Now that you know what is possible with the AL Flow State and how to access it, whether you maintain it or not is going to be a personal choice. You know what the experience feels like, and you have probably gotten a taste of what you can create and how powerful you can be. I was talking with a client the other day who told me, "I know this works when I do it but I'm struggling with making myself do the work." If this is where you are at, you are not alone. Many people need to taste their alignment, their power and influence, and then take a break. They take another lap in the struggle and push. They continue suffering until it is intense enough that their desire for change overrides their fear. Of course another option is to move into alignment, access the AL Flow State, and feel the clarity. Then, when it feels like a lot of work, instead of taking another lap in suffering you can have a virtual experience. You can see what you would create if you allowed yourself to slide back into your old way of being, at least as far as you can with your new understanding of what is possible. You can learn the lesson without engaging in the suffering and choose to commit to your routines and your alignment instead.

We have all participated in a workshop or read a book and felt the excitement and possibilities of what we could create with this new understanding. We have also all experienced being lulled to sleep again as we settled back into our old worlds. Our baseline may have moved slightly, but we let go of the opportunity for massive growth. Here we are in the final chapter of this book. You are about to read the final words. What will you choose to do with them? Will you use this book as a reference guide and fully embrace living in the AL Flow State? Will you seek out support from an Aligned Living coach? Will you just hold good intentions to change and see if anything happens? The only change that will happen is the change you commit to.

It's not complicated. When you are sovereign, entrained internally, and operating in the AL Flow State, everything is different. You think differently, operating from a higher perspective. You feel good about who you are and see yourself with clarity. It feels good to simply be in your body. Other people feel better around you or avoid you entirely. Your boundaries take care of themselves, and you call in life experiences that support you to become a better and more authentic you every day. Life can feel magical, and when you balance that magical feeling with discernment, you become a powerful architect in your life.

What I described is what most people say they want for themselves. It is all right here and available to you. The only cost is upfront. It is in having the courage and conviction to move past your fears and live in alignment. You get to choose whether you live in the high-end penthouse suite or the nasty motel on the corner. The cosmic joke is that the rent is the same price. You just need to decide whom you are going to pay it to. Until it is an ingrained habit, you need to make that choice every day. High-end penthouse suite or nasty motel on the corner?

Some days you will choose to live in the nasty motel on the corner. When we realize what we chose, and then move back into the penthouse suite, it makes it that much more enjoyable and powerful. We realize we really are choosing. We are creating. We are the architects of our reality. What will you design? What will you build?

You already have the templates for your routines. Have you filled them out? Have you reevaluated what works for you and what does not? Have you revised your routines to make them something that supports you and that you can commit to? Do you have an accountability partner that is at least as committed to the process as you are? This is an important time to be completely honest with yourself. In order to give yourself the greatest chance of stabilizing in this new way of being you need to take the steps that will support you. Go into your alignment and ask your intuitive self what you most need to put in place to assist you. Use your discernment to feel if this is an authentic truth. Then take action and step forward.

With all the different transformative work I have participated in and lead over the years, this system provides the most substantial and supportive shifts I have come across. I want you to have the same experience I have seen hundreds of clients have. At the same time, it is up to you. You now have the basic tools and understanding to move forward. The next steps and the amount of support that serves you best are something only you truly know. I wish you the best on your journey moving forward. Know that my coaches at Aligned Living and I are here to provide support if you feel one of our programs is in alignment for you.

APPENDIX I

ALIGNED LIVING SIX-WEEK PROGRAM APPLICATION

Thank you for taking the time to complete this application. Keep in mind there are no wrong answers. This is about getting in touch with where you are operating from right now. Please be open and honest with your answers. They will provide you and your potential coach insight into whether this program is the right fit for you. Any information you share will be treated with the highest level of respect and confidentiality.

Name: _____

What drew you here to work with an Aligned Living coach?

What are your top three challenges in life right now?

What are your top three successes in life right now?

List the three to five most influential relationships in your life right now.

Explain how each relationship feels supporting to you and how it feels challenging to you.

Rate your level of fulfillment on a scale of 1-10 for:

Home Life:

Work Life:

Social Life:

How committed would you describe yourself to your own personal growth?

APPENDIX II

BREAKING EXTERNAL ENTRAINMENT VISUALIZATION (ACCESSING SOVEREIGNTY)

Free audio recording available at
www.insightinfluenceandflow.com

1) Settle yourself into a comfortable space sitting with your back straight.
2) Bring your awareness out to everything around you. Take a moment to see what you feel as you let yourself expand out beyond your body. Put your hands out with your palms open. Visualize the palms of your hands as sensors that are picking up on the emotions of everybody your electromagnetic field comes in contact with. We will refer to this part of your EMF as your emotional body.
3) As you get a sense of what you are picking up on from others, ask your emotional body to rise up and separate from the rest of your EMF.

4) Then close your hands into a fist and visualize all of the sensors in your emotional body shutting down and temporarily turning off.

5) With your hands still closed in a fist, slowly bring them down to your lap. Breathe deeply and feel yourself become relaxed into this more sovereign state of being.

APPENDIX III

ACCESSING YOUR ALIGNED LIVING FLOW STATE

Free audio recording available at
www.insightinfluenceandflow.com

1) Begin with the sovereignty visualization to let go of anything you may be entrained with outside of yourself.

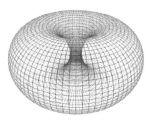

2) Instead of reopening externally, like we did when we finished the original sovereignty exercise, this time we will open internally. With your fists still closed, place one hand over your heart and the other just below your ribcage over the area known as the solar plexus. Visualize your hands representing sensors for your emotional body. As you feel ready, open your hands and use your

imagination to "see" each of your emotional body sensors reopening internally.

3) Take a moment to observe your experience. What do you notice? Use this time to bring your awareness into feeling yourself align with your spine. Then ask your consciousness to show you the alignment of the EMF of the earth. Ask to become aware of the energy of the earth's EMF starting to run in through the top of your head. Visualize and feel this energy running all the way down your spine and out your tailbone into the earth, right down through the pole of the earth. As you "see" the energy move completely through the earth, invite this same energy to run back up through your spine and out the top of your head letting it follow the alignment of the earth's EMF. Become aware of your own EMF aligning and becoming entrained with that of the earth's.

4) We will now utilize this energy to charge our body and entire EMF. Move your attention to your heart. (Not your literal heart, but where your heart lines up with your spine in the center of your body.) We will invite this flow of energy to come in through the heart and fill this whole area around your heart, chest, shoulders, spine, back, and shoulder blades. Invite the energy to move out your arms, to your elbows, then forearms, wrists, hands, and fingers. As you get a sense of fullness through this whole area of your body invite this energy to come up from the earth and through your tailbone and spine to fill this same entire area around your heart. If at any point throughout this visualization you feel like the energy is getting stuck and not flowing through you, simply move your attention to the top of your head and watch the energy flow in. Then move your attention to the base of your spine and watch the energy flow in. It should be like filling a bathtub. You

just turn on the tap and watch it fill. I find that once you reconnect with the flow, the energy will start to move again where it had felt blocked. As you feel this step complete, give permission for this energy to start to radiate out from you. Stay centered in your body and sovereignty as you send your EMF radiating out from your body. Visualize this radiating energy becoming a big sphere of light and sharing this powerful aligned energy with everybody and everything around you. Be very intentional in not following this energy so you remain internal rather than starting to re-entrain with the external.

5) Move your focus down your spine to your solar plexus (the area just below your rib cage aligned with your spine). Repeat the same steps of inviting this energy through the top of your head, and give it permission to fill all through your ribs. Then invite the energy to flow up through the tailbone filling this same space. Once you get a sense that your solar plexus has filled with this energy, give it permission to join the sphere of light around your heart. Let the energy start to radiate out, as you stay centered in it.

6) Move your focus further down your spine to just below your naval. This area is known as the sacral region. Repeat the steps of filling your sacral region and all your internal organs with this energy, coming in through the top of your head and then up through the base of the spine. Invite the sphere of light around the heart and solar plexus to expand to include your sacral and radiate out from your body while you stay aligned and centered in it.

7) Move your attention further down your spine to your root (the area at the base of your spine). Repeat the steps above including running the energy down your legs and out the base of your spine, filling your own center channel or "pole" that aligns with the earth's, allowing the

energy flowing down your spine to become one with the energy flowing through the pole of the earth.

8) Move your attention to your throat and repeat these same steps.

9) Move your attention to your head now and repeat these same steps. Quite often people feel a sense of moving from the front of the brain to feeling much more relaxed and at ease as they slide to the back of the brain and spinal column. This is the point where the sense of moving into the AL Flow State most often starts to become apparent.

10) Move your attention to the very top of your head to the space known as your crown. Repeat the same steps and feel the energy continue above your head, tying in with the pole of the earth's EMF.

11) In the final step we will become aware of the toroidal field that our EMF creates, just like the earth's. Visualize your EMF gathering at the top of your crown, running down your spine, out the base of your tailbone, and then flowing around the outside of you and back through your crown. This continuous flow is the natural formation all EMFs take. Most people feel a sense of their energy instantly feeling less chaotic and more organized.

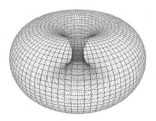

12) Connect with you spinal column, bringing your focus to the place where your brain and spine connect. Feel the energy flow through this space. Follow it down the spine

and connect with the tailbone. Use the brain stem, spine, and tailbone as your internal reference points. We can use them to replace the external reference points we would use to get our bearings. As we entrain with these internal reference points, we are no longer externally influenced in the same way.

APPENDIX IV

ALIGNED PERSPECTIVE TECHNIQUE

1) Enter the AL Flow State.
2) Pick the topics or people you want to check in on.
3) Get in touch with the flow of electromagnetic energy coming through your body. Bring your focus to how it feels as it runs through your brain and brain stem. Feel yourself moving to the back of the brain as you allow yourself to relax into this flow.
4) Use your imagination to invite the person or situation into your energy field. Stay entrained with your own electromagnetic field as the person or situation shows up. Be careful not to go into what you feel you already know, or the story you have already formed. Just observe, like you are watching a movie and have no idea what is going to happen. Don't even speculate, just see what shows up.
5) How does the person or situation appear to you? Does it seem smaller or bigger than you thought? Does it feel in or out of resonance to you? What do you notice that is different from your existing story? At this stage, the clarity usually comes in quickly.

APPENDIX V

CHOOSING YOUR BALLOONS EXERCISE

1) Complete the full Aligned Living visualization.
2) Settle into a meditative state as you get in touch with where your EMF runs through your brain and spinal column.
3) Ask your intuitive self to show you where you have been putting your energy.
4) Identify each place you have been putting your energy as a separate balloon and label it.
5) Bring the balloon into your alignment and see how it shows up for you. Does it feel in complete alignment? Then visualize yourself continuing to fill it and stay entrained with it. Does it feel mostly in alignment? Ask your intuitive self what needs to change about the balloon. Imagine yourself making those changes, and relabel the balloon. Does it feel completely out of alignment? See yourself letting your energy out of the balloon. Then choose to either discard the balloon or relabel and refill it.
6) Spend some time in your meditative state visualizing your thoughts and EMF shifting into this new, greater alignment.

7) Keep these balloons in your conscious awareness and check in with them throughout your day. You will start to catch yourself when you begin refilling old balloons you have committed to discarding. When you find yourself in your old pattern, just stop, choose differently, and celebrate the change you are making. Berating yourself for falling into old patterns fills a balloon with energy you don't want in your life.

APPENDIX VI

DAILY ROUTINES TEMPLATE

Morning Routine:

-Aligned Living meditation: What works best for you? A recording on your phone? Taking yourself through the meditation?

-Filling Your Balloons: Does it work best for you to write them out first? Do they just show up for you in meditation? What are the balloons that you fill every day?

-Are you adding a physical element such as yoga, stretching, or exercise?

Throughout the Day:

-What works best to remind you to check in on your alignment? Do you have natural breaks in your day? Do you check in before engaging with clients or coworkers? What is your plan?

Bedtime:

-What is your commitment to making sure you are going to sleep in an aligned state? Will you use a recording or take yourself through the meditation? Does it work best for you to do the meditation in bed or before going to bed?

ABOUT THE AUTHOR

Photo Credit: Kimberly Anderson Photography, Evergreen, CO

David Waldas, M.S.Ed. is an Executive Coach, trainer, and founder of Aligned Living. David specializes in helping clients access their Aligned Living Flow State and learn to utilize this state of consciousness to excel in their pursuits. David has now dedicated his career to teaching this access point and how to sustain it. He has a vision of how the world can change as more and more of us live in our Aligned Living Flow State and the natural shift in perspective that comes with it.

David, a native of central New York, spent most of his adult life in Golden, Colorado, and now lives in Encinitas, California with his wife Tracy and their two daughters, Olivia and Ava. To learn more about David and his work, visit his webpage at www.davidwaldas.com.

Made in the USA
Middletown, DE
12 March 2025

72545601R00115